RAYFIEL

OUT OF THE JUNGLE

THE JUNGLE BOY

outskirts
press

I would love to dedicate this story to all the children around the world who have encountered abuse in any of its numerous forms:

Whether it be mental, verbal, physical, emotional or even sexually abuse, I'm crying out loud telling you it was wrong and unfair for you to encounter such horrific pain. I want to advise you never to blame yourself or say to yourself that it was your fault that such traumatic events occurred. More over, I'm advising you to never let your weakness determine you. There is nothing greater than knowing you've encountered the worst, but you've proved to yourself, the ones you love and the world at large, that no matter what hardships come your way, you stand tall and put your best foot forward, releasing the best version of yourself. I have learned that you can't hold on to the pain and sorrow hoping that someone to feels remorse for your complication; it all starts with you fighting to get yourself up and out of that complication and into to a better place.

TABLE OF CONTENTS

Chapter 1 1

Chapter 2 9

Chapter 3 18

Chapter 4 25

Chapter 5 31

Chapter 6 39

Chapter 7 52

Chapter 8 58

Chapter 9 67

Chapter 10 77

Chapter 11 84

Chapter 12 106

Chapter 13 112

Chapter 14 116

Chapter 15 129

Chapter 16 142

Chapter 17 148

Chapter 18 170

Chapter 19 185

Chapter 20 220

Chapter 21 238

Chapter 22 254

Chapter 23 256

CHAPTER 1

"Ounga, if you don't stop going onto the back stairs, you'll keep falling down the concrete step stairs. See how your head is swollen? If you keep hitting your head, it's going to burst, and no one has the time right now to take no hard-eared child to the hospital," said Aunt Kimberly.

"Boy, if you don't stop touching that electrical wire, it'll shock you," said my grandmother.

"What you crying for, Ounga? I told you that what you don't hear, you'll feel," said Uncle Carlos.

My grandparents, aunts, uncles, and neighbors all continued to tell me how much of a bad and destructive baby I was. My parents told me no one could leave anything around because it all went right into my mouth. My grandparents said I was rushed to the hospital several times because I had been chewin' on Krazy Glue tubes, and got my tongue pasted to the top of my mouth. When relatives visited us during the Christmas season, my grandmother was always happy to tell everyone about my misadventures.

"It was last Christmas, and I had just come home with Ounga. Kimberly, Carlos, and Bryan were out shopping for Christmas decorations in Georgetown, the capital of Guyana. Now, I'm in the kitchen baking chicken and making pepper pot, so I set him down in the living room because I didn't want him getting himself burned in the kitchen. Then, as I'm cooking, there's an explosion followed by a scream. Right away, I drop everything and run to see what happened.

"There, laughing under the dining table, was Ounga. Just to make sure everything was okay, I turned him over and give him a quick check. His finger was grayish, smelling like smoke, and he kept pointing towards the electrical outlet behind the television."

My relatives cracked up.

"What you think happened?" Grandma asked. "He was playing with the TV plug and got shocked, the force of it sent him flying underneath the table."

My grandfather and my uncle, the one who did the wiring, told my grandmother that my being shocked was a regular show, and they could count on it whenever I was left alone.

For fifteen years, I have lived with my grandparents on the East Bank of the Demerara River opposite the Big Mediterranean House. From the time I was conscious enough to know myself, my grandmother was always a busy woman, especially when it came to church. Everyone I knew called my grandmother Sister M, but I called her Mommy.

To ensure our electricity, water, gas, and phone bills were paid, my grandmother cleaned for a few people in Georgetown during the morning, and she cooked for the church in the afternoons. My grandfather worked for a goldsmith in Stabroek Market, also located in Georgetown. Aunt Kimberly and Uncle Carlos also lived with my grandparents and me. My grandparents' two oldest son's, Scott and Bryan, and my mother, Jill, was already living their separate lives. My mother is the first-born of my grandmother's children, then Scott, Bryan, Aunt Kimberly, and then Uncle Carlos.

Whenever I would be rude to Aunt Kimberly, she always reminded me how I used to stay calm or fall asleep. "The only way I would get you to sleep was to put your face under my arm, or sometimes give you my breast to suck."

Aunt Kimberly said I didn't attend daycare. Instead, I went with my grandmother to work when they were in school. In the afternoons after school, my aunt collected me from my grandmother and took me home with her. For as long as I could remember, whenever my aunt came to take me home, there was always a problem, some big commotion over leaving. After a while, I got so attached to her that whenever I cried or needed to be put to sleep, she was the person everyone relied on. Kimberly said when I used to suck on her little breast, she never knew what I was getting, but it did a good job of putting me to sleep.

When I started out going to St. Peter's Nursery School, I used to get up at four in the morning to travel with my grandmother. St. Peter's Nursery was not too far from one of my grandmother's clients. Before Kimberly was old enough to take me to and from school, my grandmother took care of it even though I got there far too early. Grandmother always left me with the guardsman until school started. When school over, I waited with the head teacher until my grandmother arrived from work.

One night, while my grandfather was watching the news, there was an incident at another school where one of the guards had sexually abused a boy and a girl. My grandmother said she would rather I leave late with my grandfather and be late for school, than to be troubled by some guard she would then have to kill.

Other children who attended St. Peter's Nursery had their mother or father to pick them up, hug them, kiss them, and hold their hand while walking down the road. It made me miss my mother. Whenever she came to visit us, I begged her to stay with me, but she always promised she would return. On the other hand, I had my grandmother, but I was curious what it would feel like to have my parents.

One day while at school, there was a boy with a matching Spider-Man action figure and car. The boy was in my class and played with his toy during playtime. Then, the boy left his car on the table in front of me and went to use the bathroom. There were just couple of other students in the classroom, since most of the children went outside to play on the playground. I looked around just to make sure whoever was there didn't notice what I was doing, then I leaned over my desk to the boy's seat in front of me, snatched his car, and shoved it into my bag. About three minutes later, the boy returned and looked for the car.

The boy came to me first and asked if I saw his car, but I told him I thought he took it when he left the classroom. Part of me wanted to give him the car back, but I had no toys of my own and was desperate for something to play with; a toy truck was the last thing my grandparents could have afforded to buy. About thirty minutes later, school ended and his parents came for him. He was crying for his car, and his father told him they would buy him a new one. The boy settled and they left. Finally, I could play with the car the way I wanted to, but when my grandmother arrived, she saw me with the toy.

"Ounga, what it is that you have there?"

"A car, Mommy."

"Let me see it. Where did you get it from?"

"I found it."

"Where did you find it?"

I hesitated, not knowing what to say.

"Where did you find it?" she asked, as though she already knew what I did.

I took a deep breath and then said, "I found it on the floor."

"Okay," said my grandmother while staring at me.

For a second I told myself that everything is all right because my grandmother believed what I said. As we walked out of the school compound, Mommy stopped and asked me if I was sure that I had found the car.

Over the years living with my grandmother, I learned that if you tell her a lie, and she keeps asking you if you're sure what you said is what happened, it means she knows you're lying. She liked to give a chance to tell her the truth. Just after leaving the school compound, my grandmother stopped a random person and asked to borrow their phone.

"For what?" the person asked.

"My grandson is stealing, and I want to call the police."

The person laughed and walked off.

Then, my grandmother asked if I was ready to tell the truth. I couldn't lie. I told her the truth, and she said to me to take the truck, give it to the head teacher, and explain why I was giving it to her. That was the first and last time I ever stole anything. As we traveled home, my grandmother didn't say a word, but I felt sad about what I did. I looked at her, but she was wearing a look that said, "Now is not the right time to hug and love up like we normally do."

She usually wore it when she was upset, and this time I had upset her.

❧

The first time in my life that I wished I didn't know my parents, that somehow my grandparents could have been my biological parents, started one of the few weekends my mother came to visit. She told my grandmother that my father wanted me to visit him. When I was a baby, my grandmother would ask my father to help take care of me. He always refused.

"Maybe it's good that Simon is actually doing what he was supposed to do with Ounga all along," said my grandmother.

I was feeling a little bit uneasy. Part of me was happy to visit my father, sisters, and stepmother because I only heard about them, but the rest of me didn't want to leave. I knew I was going to miss Supply, but there wasn't anything I could have done to change their minds once they made them up. The following day, my mother came with my grandmother to pick me up from school. I thought they had decided not to send me to him because we were traveling in the same direction as if we were going home. But it wasn't long before my mother and I stopped at a village named Agricola.

Agricola is a twenty-minute drive from Georgetown, and about an hour from Supply. I was surprised that I had passed Agricola before and didn't know my father lived there. The wind carried the scent of the cane field, which was one of my favorite things about Agricola. While staying with my father, his wife, Kate, her grandmother, Faith, her daughter, Erica, and my sister, Emma, I loved going out on the veranda and looking over the cane field, which stretched as far as my eyes could see. But, my father had a serious problem, which was the first and only thing I remembered about him, from the time I met him until the night I escaped and built a path parallel to his."

CHAPTER 2

I tried to think: why do people have their names, why? Why I was named Rayfield Walker after my father, who was named after his father? My grandmother said my Mother was really in love with the man. That's why.

My father wanted me to move in with him and his family the second weekend my mother brought me to visit. I wasn't aware until she told me I wouldn't be coming home, and then she left. Every day, while I experienced abuse, I knew my mother could have eliminated my pain, but my parents had something else planned. I believed they didn't want me. And the fact that I was alive meant they enjoyed seeing me suffer. I still loved them, but I hated their presence; it demolished my own joy.

One afternoon, Kate had cooked green peas, mashed potatoes, and stewed chicken with corn for dinner. As soon as I walked into the house, I went into the bathroom to take off my uniform and put on my house clothes, before taking a seat at the dining table. I ate everything on my plate except the green peas. I told Kate I didn't like the way they tasted and then threw the peas away.

"You have to eat everything on your plate," said Emma.

"I don't like the way it tastes," I said.

"All right."

It wasn't long before my father walked through the door and said, "Where's my kids?"

"Daddy, Daddy," screamed Emma, as she and Erica ran into his arms.

"How was school today?"

"Good! We don't have any homework," said Emma.

"All right, So can we watch The Lion King?"

"No, can we watch Cinderella?"

"Yeah."

"Oh yeah! Daddy, Junior did not eat all of his food. He threw away the peas."

"Where is he?" my father demanded.

"At the table, sitting down."

"He better eat everything on that plate, or else I'll beat him like a snake," my father said, raising his voice.

"He already threw it in the bin," said Emma.

"Junior! I'm going to change my clothes, and by the time I come back out here, I want all of your food finished," said my father.

When I looked toward the living room, Emma stood there, smiling.

"I can't eat food I already threw in the bin," I said to myself.

"Junior, look out the window. What is that?" my father asked.

Immediately after I focused my attention on the question he asked, my father slapped me across the face.

"What did I tell you?" he shouted.

There was no way I could have said anything that was going to make him calm down. Kate tried, but he wasn't listing to her either. After a punch to my back and chest, I ran and hid the table. The fear didn't give me the courage to cry. As I kneeled under the table, my eyes tracked his footsteps, making sure I wasn't in his reach.

"Junior, come out from under the table," said my father.

Kate stood at their bedroom door while Erica hid behind her, holding her hands. Emma was still in the living room with a smirk on her face. For those few seconds, I lost focus and my father grabbed me by my shirt collar, pulling me out from my hiding place. My right foot caught on one of the chair legs, which had stopped my father from yanking me free.

My father began punching me in my face, shouting, "Come out! Come out!"

With the force he was using to pull me, I wiggled out from under the table, but my right foot snagged on a nail. As I cried, he dragged me onto the kitchen floor. My father opened the kitchen cupboard and told me to get inside or he would have beaten me like a snake.

"I'm sorry, Daddy. I won't do it again. I'll eat all of my food!" I cried.

"I'm not going to ask you again. You don't want me to get the belt."

"Come on, Simon. Give him a chance. Look, put him in the chair to sit down," said Kate.

"No, he has to learn when he doesn't hear, he will feel." My father turned to me. "Get into the cupboard and don't make a sound."

The cupboard was dark and drips of water fell on top of my head from the kitchen sink. As I sat in the cupboard, I heard rats squeaking, but it was too dark to see them. Every now and then I heard them rustle around. First, far away and then closer, a single squeak then a bunch of squeaking. After a long time, my injured foot started to burn from the dripping water. As small as I was, it was very uncomfortable to sit on my butt in the cupboard with my back against the back of the cupboard and my knees folded in front of me. After what felt like hours, I heard my father say to Kate and the girls, "I'm going to the store."

Less than five minutes after he left, I heard someone coming toward the kitchen. Kate opened the cupboard and told me not to make a sound.

"Sit right in front of the cupboard door, just in case he comes back," she said.

With the tears in my eyes and a few running down my face, I looked at her and nodded.

Kate returned to the living room and I took off my shirt, wring out the water, and used it to dry the rest of me. Then, Kate suddenly ran into the kitchen.

"You have to get back in there now. Simon is coming."

I jumped up and hurried back into the cupboard.

With the door closed behind me, I heard footsteps come closer, and then Emma opened the cupboard door and told me Daddy was calling me.

"Junior," my father called with a loud voice.

I thought the sound came from the living room, but he and Kate were in their bedroom. As I walk out of the kitchen and got closer to their bedroom, I heard his voice get clearer. When I peeked in, he was lying on one side of the bed with his leather belt around his neck while Kate lay on the other side.

"Hey, clown, come here," my father said.

I walked over to him, and he slowly took the belt from his neck and wrapped it around his wrist and palm starting with the buckle, leaving one foot of the belt length hanging.

"Smell this belt."

I leaned forward and sniffed.

"How does it smell?" he asked.

"I don't know."

"Don't worry. By the time I'm finished with you, you'll know exactly what it smells like," said my father.

Behind me, Emma burst out in laughter.

"Go to bed, and don't let me hear a sound or see you for the rest of the night," my father said to me.

"Yes, Daddy," I said, turning around and heading to the girl's room.

The girl's bedroom had two bunk beds. They said the top bunk of the bed Emma slept in was to be mine for as long as I was going to be with them. Whenever I heard my father say something belonged to me, my stomach always hurt. Without any sense of control, I was afraid.

I spent most of the night crying myself to sleep,

hoping my grandmother was going to collect me, but she never showed up. The following day, as I got up and prepared for school with the girls, my father told me to stay home. Shortly after, Erica's father came with his mini bus to collect her and Emma. Daddy warned me not to leave my chair.

"Before you think about disobeying me and coming out of that chair, think about what I will do to you when I get home. If you want, I can put you into the cupboard right now before I leave for work, and you won't come out until I get home from work. So, what you going to do?"

"I'm going to behave myself, Daddy."

"Okay, let's see."

The chair I was commanded to sit in was an old wooden chair placed in their living room opposite the comfortable sofa. Daddy took a nail and carved my name on the chair handle just so I wouldn't be confused about where my place was. On the inner back of my chair were a bunch of little nails that stuck out and pricked me whenever I sat in it.

Maybe Kate was as afraid of him as I was, because in order for her to go against my father's orders, it had to be something detrimental. As I sat in pain after my father left, Kate came into the living room, crying, and sat down on the sofa. She cried harder as she focused her attention on me.

"Junior, come." She waved me over to her.

"I can't. Daddy, don't want me to leave this chair, or else I will have to go into the cupboard when he come home."

"Don't worry. You won't go into the cupboard. I won't tell him you have left the chair."

I didn't want to continue telling her no; my grand-mother always said it was highly rude and disobedient, for a child to do the opposite of what someone older asked. I started to shake my head, but as she bowed her head and cried like I had after being beaten, I reconsidered and did what she asked. As I got out the chair and walked over to her, tears streamed her face as she tried to quickly wipe them away. "It's okay."

Kate then asked me to turn around, and she rubbed my shoulders and arms down to my elbow, then her hands rubbed down my back.

"Oh my god," she said, "your whole back is bruised."

Kate told me return to the chair while she went into her room and cried. As old as Faith was, she made it out of her bedroom and through the house by holding on to the furniture and the shelves on the walls. While standing in front of Kate's and my father's bedroom door, seeking the next object to use for support, Faith looked at me, her mouth moving. I know she wanted help to get to the chair, but I tried to tell her I couldn't move from the chair.

A moment later, Faith gave it her all and tried to reach for my chair handle and fell. If the two front legs of the chair didn't lift off the ground and smack back down with a sharp, hard sound, Kate would have never been aware of Faith's fall. Kate tried to help her grandmother up, but Faith smacked Kate's hands away, her arms shaking as she struggled to push herself back to her feet. It was clear to Kate and me that Faith was angry with Daddy for beating me and at Kate for allowing it. Whenever my father took my beatings too far, Faith would bite her lip until it bled. Some nights I could hear her crying, but for what, only God knows.

In my quiet moments, all I did was say a little prayer my grandmother taught me when I was afraid of the dark. She said God would always protect me through the words.

"God, please help me," I whispered.

CHAPTER 3

After meeting my father for the first time and then spending two days and one night in his house, I grew to fear him more than anything else that had ever scared me. Daddy made me believe it was my fault, that he had a reason to punch, kick, and slap me, when I started peeing in the bed from the nightmares I had of him beating me. Sometimes it was just a dream, but other times I was beaten out my sleep; accused for something I hadn't done but was being blamed for anyway. Instead of Supply being my home, it became the place I visited on the weekend. Every Friday, my mother came to Agricola after work and took me home. Bright and early Monday morning, she dropped me back so I would be able to travel with Erica's father.

During the second time my mother returned me to my father's house, when my mother and I were walking down the street back to his house, I told her I didn't want to go back to Daddy's because he beat me bad. I told her he locked me in the cupboard and the drum. She told me not to worry, that she would talk to him, but I continued telling her I didn't want to go.

Her exact words were, "Stop behaving like an idiot."

I cried and wiped my eyes before we reached his doorstep. I told her not to say anything because he would beat me for it. When we arrived, Kate was in the kitchen preparing lunch for the girls while they were in the backyard bathing. She said Daddy was supposed to be on his way back from the store with tennis roll, a delicious Guyanese bread roll.

While I was in the bedroom unpacking my clothes, I heard my mother telling my father that I was crying to go back to Supply and that I hadn't wanted to come back. Immediately after hearing those words, I became sleepy, and my hands, feet, and face went numb.

A moment later, she said goodbye to everyone, and came by the bedroom door and told me, "Don't cry next weekend and you will get to go back." Then, she took off.

I looked at him, and he wanted to kill me. He sent Emma in the room for his leather belt, while he called for me from where he was standing. The hair on my skin stood up, my heart beats rapidly, my eyes couldn't focus on what he was saying, and I felt sleepy.

"Come here!" he shouted, sounding like Mufasa in The Lion King. I grab my penis from outside my pants and dance in place, saying I needed to pee.

"Shut up and come."

I peed my pants right there in front of everyone in the living room. He charged into me and within second I was on the floor, screaming. Punches and slaps, one after the other, rained down on my face and stomach.

"Shut up," he screamed as he continued.

I bit my lips, trying not to make a sound, but he was slamming my head against the floor.

In the midst of my father's ferocious voice, I heard Kate crying and shouting, "Simon, stop! Simon, please stop! That's enough!"

Not a single thing on earth could have stopped him. I lay on the floor begging' for my life as a monster was trying to take everything I had. Erica's father had arrived to pick us up, and they told the two girls to go ahead and leave without me.

"Junior, it's coming."

I was sent to sit in my chair for a while. Before he left for work, he sent me to my bed, never to be seen by anyone for the rest of the day, not even by Faith who was in the same room, "Or else you'll be beaten like a snake again," said Daddy.

I couldn't make it up to the top bunk; my entire body was in terrible pain, and bruised black and blue. I took a sheet and covered myself so Faith couldn't see me, then fell asleep. Some nights, I would get up while everyone, except Faith, was sleeping and look out the window. I enjoyed gazing at the stars and the moon, wondering what was happening up there and thinking that, maybe someday I'll go on a plane and see it better.

***

"Junior," my father said, "you know you're the duncest child I have. Every one of my children, love to read or spell and work math problems. You're the only one that has a big head, and it's full of shit."

I didn't know what to say, so I smiled along with him, but it only proved how much of a fool he thought I was. The following weekend, I didn't complain about my father. I tried my best to make it seem as though my time with my father had gotten better after the first time. It was hard pretending to be happy in Supply knowing that in two days I would have to return to Agricola, where I hoped every week that things would change. My grandmother decided to take me with her to work that Saturday; she wanted to spend as much time with me before I returned.

Mommy cleaned for a woman named Ms. Daisy. I loved to follow her to work when she was going to Miss Daisy's home. Ms. Daisy had a twenty-two-year-old son named Alan. Right after helping my grandmother clean

Ms. Daisy's bathtub and mopping her stairs, Alan and I would sit and watch Cinderella, Peter Pan, Pinocchio, Tarzan, and the best of them all The Lion King. Every time Alan and I watched The Lion King, I cried. He never understood why I cried, and I didn't explain it to him. My father loved to watch The Lion King with his family; every time he played the DVD, I was either told not to look at the television by turning my face or was sent out of the room.

Everyone in his household had a character they were. Daddy was Mufasa, Kate was Sarabi, Erica was Zazu, Faith was Rafiki, and Emma was Pumbaa. I was supposed to be Simba, but Daddy said he needed another son to be Simba. He said I wasn't qualified. Watching it with Alan, I could be who I wanted to be. The day after was church, then came Monday through Friday. I started to prepare myself for whatever beating I had to receive.

"No matter how much he beat me, I will not cry—but I might die," I said to myself.

That week, Kate's eldest brother, Dave, was there with a computer he was trying to sell and a suitcase full of clothes. He told Kate he just needed somewhere to stay for a couple of months, but he ends up leaving before two weeks were up.

The first time Dave saw my father lift me out of my chair and slam me into the wall, holding me by my neck, he cursed my father, telling him how fucking cruel he was. For the time that Dave was there in Agricola with us, I felt at ease. Daddy would turn from beating me to arguing with Dave, but when my father insulted Dave, telling him how much of a junkie he was, and the girls complained that he smelled, it hurt him. Dave got angry and left, never to return to Agricola. It was true that he smelled, but it didn't bother me; at times, I smelled worse.

While hurrying to finish my tea one morning, I dropped the cup because it was too hot. My father ran out his room curious to find out what happened. After I explained the situation to him, he went into his room and quietly returned with his leather belt.

I was beaten until I urinated myself. Then I was punched and kicked for peeing my uniform. I couldn't attend school, and much of my body— my face, lip, arms, and back—were black and blue or swollen.

"God, please don't make Daddy beat me," I prayed.

Daddy said the lash would be powerful if he got to stretch the belt out.

"Stand back because if this belt hits me, every lash you're supposed to get will be tripled."

"I'm sorry, Daddy. I won't do it again."

He held the belt from the buckle while the body of the leather belt hung in the air over his shoulder; then, he fired a lash. The lashes stung and I tried not to cry. Daddy whined, mocking me, and asked if it hurt. I told him I needed to pee, but he couldn't have cared less while I stood in front of him, holding my penis to prevent myself from peeing. After a few minutes, I let go; my skin was burning, bruised, and hurting. I was put into the drum beside the cupboard for peeing on myself. Although inside the drum was really dark because Daddy covered it, I was happier to be in there than to continue being beaten. I drifted off to sleep, and when I woke, I was in the top bunk.

CHAPTER 4

K ate's nephew, Aron, was about four years older than me and he teamed up with Emma. Some days after school when I was told to stand and put my face to the wall, Daddy used to play fight with Aron. Daddy loved to tickle and throw the other kids up in the air in the front yard. In that same front yard, there was a large hook where daddy would hang me from my shirt collar, and they would all stand back and laugh till I was taken down. The boys at school would talk about their older brothers, and how they played video games and hung out with their friends. I had told myself that if I had an older brother, he would protect me. My mind changed when I met Aron.

While preparing for school one morning, everyone, including myself, was in a hurry from waking late. My father normally woke us up, but due to the fact he went to bed late, everyone slept in. We had half an hour to prepare until Uncle Jones arrived, which meant everyone had to finish bathing, getting dressed, and eating break-fast. Everyone except Aron was warned to finish bathing by the time Daddy returned from the grocery store. There wasn't any bread or sugar, so he went to buy them. The minute Daddy walked out the door, it became survival of the fastest.

As a result of the upstairs bathroom pipe not work-ing, we all had to go out into the backyard to bathe. I was supposed to bathe before the girls and Aron. I ran down the stairs and made it to the stand pipe before they did, but Emma told me Kate said Erica and her should hurry so they could help her prepare lunch. After a while of refusing to give her the bathing container, the girls fought me for it. They said not to worry, that I was going to bathe right after them. In the meantime, I brushed my teeth. When Emma was finished, she gave Aron the bath-ing bowl and told him to hurry up. Aron looked at me, laughing as he moved in slow motion to throw the water on his skin. Emma stood on the stairs and giggled. Again, she told him to hurry, then ran upstairs. Immediately af-ter Aron finished, I collected the container and hurried to bathe. Every now and then as I dipped the water out of the bucket to wet my skin, I looked front, back, left, then right. I thought the coast was clear, but in the pro-cess of soaping my face I heard my father running down the stairs. I tried not to panic because I didn't want to get burned. Before I could dip another jug of water, the lash came from the left, right, back, and front.

When the leather belt collided with my wet skin, the lashes burned and I rolled on the floor and cried, "Daddy, please stop!"

He didn't stop or listen, instead he continued to use his power to beat me like a snake. My eyes burned from the soap and my hot tears, and I couldn't do anything but take whatever was given. Later, he paused and told me to get up.

"I can't. My eyes are burning."

"You want me to show you how fast you can get up?"

"No, Daddy, my eyes is burning," I cried while I stumbled to my feet.

"Rub your eyes," he said while he threw water at my face.

Eventually, the burning stopped, and he told me to go upstairs, "Don't pass the kitchen."

I did exactly what he said and waited by the cupboard. Right behind me, he opened his fifty-five gallon plastic barrel and told me to get inside. Emma and Aron smiled and then walked away. Kate stood by her bedroom door, crying. Her eyes flicked between the barrel and me clinging to the wall.

"Simon, you don't have to do this. Spare him," said Kate.

"Kate, relax your-fucking-self. I have to teach this boy a lesson."

"Come on. At least let him dry his skin," she begged as tears ran down her face.

"It's like you cunt don't understand English!" he yelled at Kate. Then he looked into my eyes, lifted me up, and put me inside the barrel. Before he covered the barrel, he told me to sit and said, "If I only hear a sound, I'm locking this drum with a padlock."

Before he walked away, Daddy covered the barrel and pounded the side. I screamed, scared because the inside was too dark. He hit the cover again, and from the inside I heard the lid click. Instead of going to school, I spent the whole, entire day in the barrel. Part of the time, I slept, but it was very exhausting. It was a very hot day, and I sweated like a glass of ice cold Coke chilling in the sun on a beach day. The only thoughts that ran through my mind were, What's happening? When is this going to end? God, please help me.

Since I was the only boy who lived there, Aron only visited. Taking out the garbage was my job. No one ever had to tell me more than once to take the trash bag downstairs; the only problem was the dark. I was terrified of the dark.

The main garbage bin was under the back stairs, and whatever little trash we accumulated had to go into the main dumpster by the end of the night, according to the landlord. From the time I started walking down the stairs, I sang loud enough for Kate to hear me. Just in case there was someone in the dark waiting to kill me. They would have think twice because Kate would realize I stopped. Around that time, Kate was usually washing the dishes and making sure the house was tidy before going to bed. One evening while I was singing, my father came out on the back patio and told me that when I was finished singing, I should come upstairs and sing for him. Immediately, I shut my mouth. I didn't mind staying downstairs, silent in the dark.

"God, please help me," I prayed.

"Oh! You're quiet now? You don't want me to come down there for you."

"I'm coming."

I prepared myself for what was to come. I looked on the bright side. If he put me in the barrel, my skin wasn't wet and I wouldn't sweat because it was a cool night outside.

I went upstairs. There was a chair in the kitchen. Sitting on the chair was my father.

"I can see you're feeling happy tonight, but you wanna see me make you unhappy."

"No, Daddy."

"Yeah, man, there must be a reason why you're happy.

You not supposed to feel so happy. Come, I think you need to chill out in the drum."

"No, Daddy, I'm sorry."

"What you told me? No. You want me to get the belt?"

"No."

"Then come on."

As I sat in the barrel for a few hours, I heard Aron and Emma creeping around the drum, giggling. As hard as it was to ignore them, I convinced myself that they weren't against me, and I became my own best friend. I started talking to myself, asking questions and answering them. That's how I got the nickname Crazy and Doltish. In Supply, I used to talk to and beat the trees in our backyard because they never listened to anything I said.

CHAPTER 5

One afternoon, I refused to board Uncle Jones's bus. I was expecting my mother or grandmother to pick me up after school, but neither one of them showed up. I stood in front of the school, leaning my head on the fence, hoping my grandmother would show up. But no matter how far I looked down the road, there wasn't any sign of her.

"Big head! Come on the bus," said Emma.

"She's coming. She always comes," I cried.

Uncle Jones told me he was going to call my father if I didn't board the bus, which was how I got on board.

"When we reach home, I'm going to make Daddy beat you," said Emma.

As Uncle Jones drove away from the school, I looked down every corner—left, right, front, and back—to see if she was running late. Maybe Mommy had forgotten to pick me up.

"You better prepare yourself. Daddy will beat you like a snake," Emma said, laughing with her friends on the bus.

"Cry a baby, Jojo. Put ya finger in ya mouth and tell ya mother why ya crying', boo fa ya."

"When I get home, I'm going to tell my grandmother on you," I said.

"I don't care because when we get home, Daddy will beat you, then put you in the cupboard," replied Emma.

I shut my mouth and leaned my head against the window as my heartbeat increased.

"Mommy is probably at Daddy's house waiting on me to go home," I whispered. "Please, God, make my grandmother wait on me until I reach Daddy's."

When we arrived home, I was hoping my grandmother was there and scared of Emma complaining about me. The second I reached upstairs I asked Kate if my grandmother or mother had come to pick me up. She told me my father said I had to stay for the weekend. Kate cooked, but I didn't have the appetite to eat anything. My next move, after hearing I wasn't going home, was to prepare myself to be beaten and put into the barrel. I continued to ask God not to let him beat me or put me in the barrel and lock it as much.

"Daddy, today after when Uncle Jones came to pick us up, Junior didn't want to come on the bus."

"Why you didn't want to go on the bus?"

Before I could answer, he slapped me, then told Emma to bring his leather belt.

"Take off your clothes."

Right after he collected the belt from Emma, he started lashing me across my skin with all of his might and power. Not only did I cry from the sting, whether it was my eyes, lips, back, chest, or buttocks, but from his punches and being slammed into the floor over and over. I screamed at the top of my lungs and begged him to stop, but he was too furious and disgusted by me. As much as I wanted to urinate, I was expected to hold it until Daddy had finished belting me. Along with the burning sensations from the lashes, my penis burned from holding my pee. I was happy to be thrown into the cupboard. My lip had burst. My tummy hurt. My body was covered with belt brands. Shortly after the television turned off, the sound of everyone disappeared.

That night, I dreamed I was in Supply with my grandparents. Our family was having lunch, and everyone was happy to see me when I returned home. The next morning when I woke, my eyes ran with tears. If only the dream had been real, everything from that point back to the beginning would have been a nightmare. I wished every day that he wasn't my father; I wasn't sure who else it could be, but I knew for sure anyone else would have been better. For no reason at all, I was being beaten. Out of the blue, I was punched, slapped, or kicked out of my chair. I wished for my father to die. But how was that going to happen? I didn't think or decide how, but his death would have stopped him from ill-treating me.

The next week when Kate and the girls left to visit a friend, the couple who lived downstairs came upstairs to watch the cricket game with Daddy. Guyana's cricket team, the West Indies, was playing against Sri Lanka. They were all betting that the West Indies were going to win the World Cup. But the way they were shouting, a stranger would have thought the man was for the Sri Lanka and Daddy was for the West Indies. Game after game, they got louder; I got out my chair and went on the veranda to play and talk with the birds. Daddy always had some plastic chairs stacked on top of each other beside the window just in case his friends came over and wanted to hang out.

They cheered every five to ten minutes when the West Indies scored, and I unpacked the chairs, getting ready to play. Each plastic chair was given a name. I remembered one of the chair's legs was broken, and it couldn't stand on its own; I called him Leanney because he was always leaning on another chair. There was Tally, Dusty, Blacky, and couple others. I talked to the chairs even though they never responded. The majority of the time, they had me answer the questions I asked them. The electrical wire that was connected to the house had a few Pigeons resting on it, curiously watching me interact with the chairs. Every now and then, the birds flapped their wings while hanging on the wire. As the electrical wire shook, I was asked to check it out and solve the problem.

"The birds are shaking the wire. I can't reach it, and I'm scared of the birds."

Daddy came out with the pointer broom to lash them off, but Leanney made him fall as he rushed to hit the pigeons.

"Who put these chairs like this?" Daddy asked.

"I was playing with them."

"Get inside."

The sound of his voice sent chills down my spine, but I told myself maybe I wouldn't get beat because of the visiting neighbors. I couldn't stop my heartbeat from increasing, but I begged God not let him beat me. Daddy asked the neighbors to excuse us before telling me to go in his bedroom. In front of the guests, I begged him not to beat me. He roughly grabbed me by the shoulder and pushed me into his bedroom.

"If you make a sound, I'm going to beat you so bad your skin will peel off. Now! This is what I want you to do: take off your clothes, turn your face to the wall, and don't look back."

I peed myself before he started beating me. Then, one after the other, he lashed me with his leather belt. A couple times, the belt buckle hit my head, but I tried not to make a sound. I thought I was going to be put in the cupboard, but I was sent to my chair. There was a burning sensation coming from the back of my head, and when I touched the spot, the pain increased. I looked at my fingers, and there were a couple spots of blood. I never told him that I used one of my black shirts to stop the bleeding.

I continued wishing he would die. I didn't want to be around him; I was too scared. I couldn't look him in the face. I felt the need to cry or die, and I wished I wasn't his child. Whenever I saw or heard him, even if someone mentioned his name, I got scared. I used to hope he had somewhere to go, or that he would get into a fight and the other person made him cry the way he loved to see me cry. No matter how much I hoped and wished for those things, they never came to pass. I missed my grandparents. I talked to myself about things we had talked and laughed about. Emma and Erica laughed and called me crazy, and sometimes said I was stupid. Just to make sure I didn't say anything to get myself in trouble, I asked them to leave me alone.

When Daddy wasn't around, I used to cry for my grandparents, my aunt, my uncle, and my mother. I cried and talked to myself about how much I loved and needed to see them. It was Thursday and the next day I was going up to Supply. Emma heard me saying that I couldn't wait to see my grandparents, and told Daddy when he came home. Exhausted, he said he wasn't going to beat me. Instead, I was put into the cupboard for a while.

Bright and early that Friday morning, I woke up ready to go home. I couldn't wait to see Supply. Throughout the whole day and every time I got the chance, I looked outside to see if my grandmother was there at the gate. Sometimes, she arrived before school ended, and I was lucky that day. When I saw her, I ran out of the classroom to hug and kiss her. I told how much I missed her, and that I didn't want to go back to my father's home.

Mommy didn't ask why, but she replied, "Okay."

I waited until we reached home, way past Agricola, then informed my grandmother about the way my father treated me. Immediately, her expression changed.

My mother got blamed for everything. Not because I told my grandmother that I told her and she told Daddy, which caused him to beat me, but because my mother was trying to defend him. I went into Carlos's and my bedroom to lay down. My heart was happy I was back home, but my mind kept worrying about my father finding out,

Maybe I'll have to go back to his house or something even worse, I thought. I felt overwhelmed with guilt every time my grandmother and mother argued; it was always over me. I still continued to hope my mother would become loving like my grandmother. Maybe someday when my grandmother couldn't pick me up, she would. But the only time I saw her was for the couple of hours I spent with my grandfather before he put me on a bus to go home.

CHAPTER 6

I remembered the day I asked my grandmother why my mother called my grandfather Uncle Adam. I wasn't prepared for her response, but she said I had a right to know. To this day, I thank her for being truthful. She took a deep breath in and released all of her stress before telling me the story.

"Adam is not your real grandfather. He's not your mother's father. Your real grandfather is my first husband," she said.

I understood what she said, but I didn't take it as seriously as I should have; the only thing that I cared about was that Adam Rall was going to be with me.

"Your mother and Uncle Scott are my first husband's children, and Bryan, Kimberly, and Carlos are Adam's children," she said. "Your real grandfather lives in the United States."

After hearing that story, I thought of my real grandfather.

"Mommy is crazy. Daddy is my real grandfather. I didn't see any difference; my grandfather and I look alike. I always walked behind him wherever we went. If he had a big cutlass and a fork stick, I had a small cutlass and a fork stick. When he cut down a big tree, I cut down a small one. When we got tired during the day and he drank a big coconut, I struggled with a small one until he poured it into a cup for me. When he told a joke and stuck out his tongue, I tried to say one and failed, but still stuck out my tongue. When he ate whole wheat bread, I ate white bread, and when he finished watching the news, we watched Full House."

"Mommy is probably making a joke," I said to myself. From that day on, I didn't care who Paul Joan was or where he lived.

Every afternoon, my grandmother picked me up from school and took me to the market so I could travel home with my grandfather. I observed how he walked and spoke to see if it was similar to how I did. I couldn't tell if it there were any differences. But when my grandfather and I were on our way home, his friends always shouted, "Adam! You and your son!"

My mother dated a guy named Robert who worked with my grandfather. He was cool at times, like when he complimented me on my relationship with my grandfather's and me; other times, he made me angry. He used to call me Duty Bundle. When I came from school, he always wondered if I was cleaning the school drainage or the toilet.

My mother thought it was a good idea for me to attend St. Angelus Primary because Emma, Erica, and one of Erica's cousins, Acacia, went there. While I was entering Prep A, Emma and Erica were moving over to Primary One. Acacia was in Primary Two, and her older sister, Amie, was in Primary Four and preparing to graduate. Although we were going to the same school, I made it hard for them to find me during the day. Whenever I saw either of them, I was reminded of my father, so my aim was to run away.

There was one time when I was putting up my pencils and book into my bag, and all I heard was, "Junior! Junior."

When I turned around and looked toward the school door, there were Emma and Erica. I put the bag on my back and disappeared into the crowd. I did everything I could to avoid them.

When I waited for my grandmother after school, they often waited along with me until she came. Not wanting to spend any time with the girls, I asked my grandmother if instead of waiting for her after school, could I hop on a minibus and meet my grandfather. My grandmother was scared, but my grandfather encouraged her to let me try. After a week of traveling on my own, I proved my grandfather right. The next step I took was to show him I was able to travel from Georgetown to Supply on my own, that way I could avoid Robert and my mother. For the first month and a half, Daddy insisted on putting me on a bus with a driver and conductor he knew. While my grandfather took me to the bus stop on our way home, a bus conductor he knew very well shouted, "Red Man! You going home?"

"No, not yet. It's just my grandson."

"All right, don't worry. We got him. He's in good hands," said the conductor.

"I know, just make sure he gets off at the Big Mediterranean House."

"Yeah, man, I got it. The Big Mediterranean House is right where you get off."

And just like every time he dropped me off, my grandfather gave me a kiss and hug, and then said he would see me when he got home.

During the first week of traveling on my own, I slept away the drive until the conductor woke me up five minutes before we reached my home. Sometimes, I was lucky and Uncle Carlos was home. If he wasn't, I had to stay outside and wait for Aunt Kimberly or my grandfather. I always preferred to stay with Uncle Carlos after school. He didn't pay attention, whether I finished my homework or if I was playing too much; as long as I behaved myself, everything went perfect. Aunt Kimberly was the opposite; when she helped me with my homework, anyone would've thought she was practicing to become a teacher.

I could tell whether Uncle Carlos was home the moment I got off the bus, because very loud music would be playing on the veranda. Some of the music he played I wasn't too interested in because I couldn't understand what the singer was saying. For instance, he loved listening to 50 Cent, Eminem, Busta Rhymes, and Fabulous.

Once Carlos got home, I changed my clothes and maybe listened to some of his music before straying around the neighborhood. In Supply, we had a neighbor named Jones, but everyone, including his family, called him Rum Ton. If you were looking to find Jones, the first place to check was the liquor store. My grandmother never likes it when I visited Jones, except if I going with Uncle Carlos to play cricket with his two sons, Ben and Casper.

Uncle Carlos and Ben were very good friends, and most of the time they tolerated Casper. They said he was too young, but I objected because he was way older than me. Uncle Carlos and I would go over to Mr. Jones's once in a while because his kitchen was better looking than ours. They had several boxes of different types of cookies, a lot of chocolate, box milk, cheese, fruits, soda, rum, wine, and candies. In our home, the only time we got to see all those food at once was during the Christmas season. At first, I used to only visit them with Uncle Carlos; but as they got comfortable with our family, I visited often. My grandparents didn't mind me running over there to watch television, because it was during the time we struggled with the cost of living, and blackout for our home was common. One early Saturday morning, I went over to watch television. In Guyana, the only day that cartoons showed all morning was Saturday; so I wanted to go and watch all I could.

Normally, whenever Uncle Carlos came with me, while watching the television Ben, Casper, and I would each be in our own chair. That morning, Ben sat on the arm of the chair I was sitting in.

"Go and sit down in your own chair," I said to him, but he didn't pay me any attention.

"Where's the remote?" asked Ben.

"I don't know. I think you last had it," said Casper, and got up and began looking for it. I looked in the chair I was sitting in, but it wasn't there. "I can't find it,"

"Don't worry." Ben got up, turned off the television, and returned the chair arm.

"Why'd you turn off the television?" I asked. "What happened? You want the chair?"

"No, I want you bent over that chair," said Ben as he pulled me up.

"Why?"

"Just bend over the chair. I want to show you something," he insisted.

"Why?"

"Ounga, bend over the chair arm before I stop you from coming over here."

"I think my grandmother is calling me," I said nervously.

Before I could make a move, Ben leaned me over the chair and told me to stay still as he pulled down my pants and then my briefs.

"No," I cried out.

"No! Don't get up. Just now," he said.

I felt his penis by my buttocks, and I tried to stop him. I gave him a hard time by fighting up. I tried to use my hands to cover my buttocks, but he pushed my face down into the chair, and removed my hands, hurting me. As I begged him to stop, he began to push hard and harder.

"Relax!" he said.

"My buttocks is hurting."

"Don't worry, it'll stop." He hushed me and then called out to his brother. "Casper, bring some cooking oil from the kitchen!"

"I have to go home," I said, still trying to get away.

"Just now, the oil will make it happen faster."

"It's hurting," I cried.

Ben didn't care. He pressed my head down in the chair seat and push harder and harder.

"Look, this will make it feel better."

"It's hurting bad."

"If you keep fighting up and crying, the longer I'm going to take. Just relax,"

I cried, and he continued.

When Ben finished, Casper came over to the chair and asked me to suck his penis. I cried and begged them not to make me do it. At first, Ben said he was going to stop me from visiting their home, but when he realized I kept my mind focused on going home, he held me down while Casper forced his penis by my buttock. Ben tapped me on my head and said, "Just now, you'll go home. He's almost done."

"Tell him he can't tell anyone because they'll think he's an aunty man," said Casper.

Caspar told me to stretch my hands out and collect the semen that came out of his Penis. I needed to go so I did whatever he said. After squeezing the semen completely out of his penis and into my hands, Ben pushed his penis against my face.

"Open your mouth and suck it."

"I can't."

"You want to go home?"

"Yeah."

"Then you gotta suck it nice and quick."

After Ben was finished, Casper did the same thing; they kept me there for a couple hours. The second I got home, I bathed my skin, brushed my teeth, and cleaned my ears. I dressed myself and climbed into bed thinking about what Ben and Casper did to me. During the night, I dreamed I was at Ben and Casper's home and they forced me to do it all over again. I was drenched in sweat when I woke. For the next few nights, I didn't sleep. I didn't say anything either because I didn't want Uncle Carlos and his friends to avoid me. Not long ago, when I was sitting on the back stairs, I listened in on his and his colleague's conversation.

"If I see any man that wants to be with another man, I would beat him to death," said Uncle Carlos while his friends laughed aloud.

As much as I was ashamed and overwhelmed by Ben and Casper molesting me, I was scared to tell Uncle Carlos and later anyone else even though I hadn't wanted it; they forced me. Again and again, thoughts ran through my head and said that if I told anyone, my family might not want anything to do with me. My grandmother was a very strong believer in God and the church, and she always told everyone about the Bible story of the towns of Sodom and Gomorrah. My grandmother said in the towns of Sodom and Gomorrah, men were in sexual relationships with men as well as women, so God burned the city down to the ground. The minute she started to tell the tale, my aunt always described how bad she knew it was. Time after time, I had convinced myself not to tell anyone.

The following day, when I didn't visit them, Casper came over while I was sitting on the back stairs. He told me we had to do it again. I refused, and he picked me up and carried me into our outdoor toilet.

"I promise I won't do it like Ben," he said while trying to kiss me.

Physically, I was there following his commands, but mentally I was in a field; that's what I called it. There were other children in the field, sad as though they had lost their parents. I was on the opposite side of the area, but not too far away. Not one of them noticed me or each other. It was as if every child had access, and was able to reach out to them while seeing many similar to myself. I became conscious when he forced his penis onto me. I screamed and ran out of the toilet, through the bushes beside our neighbor's yard, and down the damned river where the great fishing pond was. I sat down and leaned my head against a bamboo tree and fell right asleep.

When standing on our veranda, I was able to see all of our neighbor's homes, including Casper and Ben's. The veranda was my favorite place in our home. It also gave me a clear view of Peter Joan's home. Whenever I was home, I locked the glass door to the veranda and refused to look at Peter Joan's home. I wasn't happy going over to Casper's when we ran out of food during the week and Uncle Carlos sent me to collect some food from them; I could have told him what happened and he would have stopped being friends with them, but I would have been rejected by Uncle Carlos. There was a day where I had stayed home from school to help Uncle Carlos pick coconut. As much as we had desired to quench our thirst with coconut water on that hot day, without a cutlass, he would have had to turn to the standpipe and drink regular water. Uncle Carlos begged me to go and borrow Ben and Casper's cutlass. Just as my uncle said, I went and asked to borrow the cutlass. But before I saw Ben, I saw the cutlass, my plan was to pick it up and run back home, but Ben saw me through his bedroom window.

"Ounga, what you doing with that cutlass?"

"Uncle Carlos want to borrow it"

"So, that's the way you borrow people's stuff? Don't take that one. That one belongs to Daddy. Come, I'll give you mine."

From the front steps where I was, I saw Ben cleaning his room.

"Before you collect the cutlass, can you help me push this bed?"

"I can't Uncle Carlos needs me to come back now with the cutlass."

"It won't take long, I promise."

"Hey Ounga, what you doing? Said Mr. Jones out of nowhere.

"Uncle Carlos want to borrow a cutlass."

"Ben or Casper give Ounga a cutlass."

"I was going to give him one, but I asked him to help me and Casper to turn this bed around."

"They want you to help them with some bed."

"Okay."

I told myself that I didn't have to worry because Mr. Jones was in the yard.

"The bed has wheels, and when I push it, you just have to steer the wheel into the corner," he said.

When I walked into the room, he walked outside and closed the front door.

"The place is getting windy; I think the rain is about to fall," he said while walking back into the bedroom.

"Lay down on the bed," he said.

"No, I can't. Uncle Carlos will be mad with me."

"Why? You told him?" he asked.

"No, it's just that he said two man shouldn't do it, or he would gone kill them." I said.

"What he was talking about is something different. There's nothing is wrong with this."

"I have to go home now. Uncle Carlos is waiting on me to bring back the cutlass," I said.

"It's not going to take long. Lay down on the bed," he said. Just as I tried to escape, he pushed me onto the bed and fought me. While I tried to defend myself while he took off his pants, while his penis was erect. "Don't worry, Ounga. It's not going to take long."

I tried to rise up, but he was too heavy. I clenched my buttock, but he was pushing his penis hard and harder. I cried and begged him to stop, but he told me to calm down.

"Just now it will feel better."

"My buttocks hurts" I cried.

"It will stop just now. Just relax."

Soon after, he jumped up, pulled up his pants, told me to put on my pants, and then went out in the living room. Uncle Carlos was calling from the sand road. He wanted to know why I was taking so long. I lied to him, saying we had to look for the cutlass. Uncle Carlos believed it. His father nor Casper was nowhere to be seen.

CHAPTER 7

There was a beautiful teacher named Ms. Freedom who used to purposely pick me to solve the mathematics problems she wrote on the chalkboard, and I always told her either that I couldn't do it, or she could ask someone that knows the answer. Sometimes when Ms. Freedom gave us group work, I would sit down and pretend she didn't give me any work.

"Look at this one here. He sits back, comfortable like he's at the bar, while these other children in the group do the work," said Ms. Gloria, a fellow teacher and friend of Ms. Freedom.

"You better not come into my class and do that shit, or else the whip you see me with will be printed in your hands," she said.

Without saying a word, I looked at her as though she was crazy. There was something there. I couldn't stand them, and they couldn't stand me. Ms. Gloria told me I would guard St. Angelus someday when I become an adult. Ms. Gloria came into Ms. Freedom class one day and beat me while the students from my class and other classes close by watched and smiled.

Why had she beaten me? I never found out, but she told me it didn't make any sense, I told my father because they're good friends and he knows. When I did anything that upset Ms. Gloria she took a thick wooden ruler and beat me on my buttocks until I cried. My buttocks burned a lot, I couldn't sit when she had finished. The first time I got into a fight was with a boy named George. How the fight started, and who raised the tension, Ms. Gloria never gave me a chance to explain myself, but I kept it cool. Both George and I had yellow pencils, the only difference between them is that mine had a fine scratch; it was my signature move to catch thieves. Sometime during lunch George lost his pencil, and then after lunch, when I was fixing my book and getting ready to take notes, George looked at me and said, "I can't find my pencil. Rayfield thief it."

Ms. Gloria didn't ask any questions. She assumed it was George's pencil and told me to give it back. I tried to explain that my pencil had a scratch, but she wouldn't listen. Within a wink an eye, George leaned over and yanked the pencil out my hands. I got angry and pounded him in his face. I didn't mean to, but I punched him on his lip, and it burst. Ms. Gloria grabbed me by my shirt collar and pulled me to the main office. They didn't want to hear anything I had to say about how the situation started. Ms. Gloria told the head teacher what she believed and the principal called my grandmother. I wasn't expecting them to call my grandmother, but I was happy they didn't call my father. I was just suspended for the day.

Not long after that day, it was forty-five minutes before school was over, and I was going to the bathroom, near the back of the school when I heard someone shout, "Junior!"

Before I saw who it was, my heartbeat increased and the palms of my hands grew moist—I knew that voice. I thought my father wanted to beat me for telling my grandmother, he had beaten me when I spent time with him in Agricola.

"Why you're not in the class?"

"I'm going to the bathroom to urinate," I replied.

"Okay, go and hurry back to class," he said.

"Yes, Daddy." As I walked further away from him, I started crying.

Why? I didn't know. Something had caused me to cry, and for a while I couldn't stop. When I reached in the restroom, I didn't urinate. Instead, I wiped my eyes so no one would notice I'd been crying.

On my way back to class, Ms. Gloria was talking to Daddy in the hall. I tried to turn around and walk the other direction, but they spotted me.

"Junior, come," Ms. Gloria said. I walked over and she asked, "Who do you live with?"

"With my grandmother and grandfather."

"Do you pay attention to what Rayfield is doing in school?" asked Ms. Gloria.

"Why?"

"I think you should ask him," she said.

"Why is your teacher asking me if I pay attention to your schoolwork?"

I looked at Ms. Gloria, then responded, "I don't know."

"Miss, you hear the boy, he doesn't know." He smiled, and then she smiled.

Ms. Gloria called him aside and whispered something to him. Within a few minutes, they both started laughing. He returned to where I was standing and asked me if I wanted to know what Ms. Gloria had just told him.

"Your teacher just said the only thing you will grow up to be is a guard," then he continued laughing. "Ms. Gloria, how could you say something like that to my boy?"

"It's not like I'm lying," she replied.

They laughed while I stood there unconscious.

Soon after Ms. Gloria returned to the classroom, my father left, and I went back to the bathroom. On my way back to the class, I looked at him from the top of the school stairs, thanking God he hadn't beat me.

"Your father and me is good friends now," Ms. Gloria said. "So if you play the fool and don't do what I say, you will get whipped."

Although teachers in Guyana are allowed to beat their students, if any teacher had known or was friends with your parents, it was an easy way for them to make you do your schoolwork by beating you every time you acted foolishly. I had a friend named Derick Clark, who attended St. Angelus with me. Everyone called him Clarks, not because of his last name, but because he wore Clarks shoes. Ms. Gloria and Ms. Greene were friends, and during every lunch break, they sat, ate, and talked about all the students. Sometimes, I heard them chatting about how much some of the children loved to be beaten, "especially Rayfield Walker and Derick Clark," they said.

Both Derick and I knew he had been framed. Ms. Gloria, who was friends with his mother, called her up and lied that he wasn't doing his homework. I knew that he did his homework because I copied from him when we met before class. Something happened and he couldn't find it. It was a rainy day, so during lunch anyone who wasn't eating or drinking had to have their head on their desk. Both Derick and I had our heads down, whispering how much the teachers loved to chit-chat.

"Get up! You lil' piece of shit," a woman shouted.

Everyone who wasn't eating, including Derick and I, looked up.

"Take off your belt now," the woman said.

The way Derick slowly got up, the look on his face gave it all away. He took off, running around the furniture, dodging her as she swung the belt. Some of the students moved to avoid being hit.

I went outside and sat on the stairs until they were finished. After a while, the woman came out the classroom and went to the main office with Derick. As they walked, groups of students were walking behind Derick as though he was Jesus and they were his followers. Some were crying for and with him. Others were saying, "Aunty, don't beat him."

Ms. Gloria and Ms. Greene giggled, smiled, and laughed.

When I reached the market, I told Robert and my grandfather about Derick and what his mother did to him.

Robert smiled and said, "If he's not doing what he's supposed to do, then there will be consequences."

When I told him, Derick was running all over the classroom, he sat there and laughed until his eyes got red and his tummy hurt.

CHAPTER 8

I t was a Sunday afternoon when my grandmother was cooking lunch that I asked her, "Mommy how come Mommy and Daddy are not together like you and Daddy."

Clearly, I'd seen it.

My grandmother took a deep breath and asked me why I loved to ask so many questions. Then she said, "Your father is not an ordinary man. He used to beat your mother terribly bad while they were together, and was always pinching you until you cried. When your mommy Jill was pregnant with your younger sister Lina, he kicked her down the stairs. Never wanted to contribute to anything that you needed."

My grandmother was always talking about the milk. For as long as I could remember, my grandmother always emphasized how hard my father made it to bring milk. She said he never brought it.

"They both was young, and couldn't afford to keep you guys. So, your father took Emma, and you and Lina went with his mother. But every now and then, your mother and I had to take you to the hospital because you were getting sick. One day we noticed that everything was fine when she brought you to our house in the village. It was the first time in one week you weren't vomiting, didn't have a fever, or diarrhea. The day you returned home, straight back to the hospital we went again. So I told her to bring you here to stay, and from that moment, you didn't visit the hospital or their home."

That night I sat down and thought about everything she told me. There were a lot more questions I wanted to ask her, but I didn't think I was ready for the answers.

The Big Mediterranean House and Peter Joan were the talk of our village. Damion, one of the caretakers of the house, who soon became my aunt's husband, introduced Peter's life to us.

When we were sitting on our back stairs one night, Damion said, "Peter Joan's name was Riley Joan before he changed it. As an only child growing up with his mother and father, Peter Joan couldn't attend school because his parents couldn't afford it.

Although they were poor, every morning when Peter woke, he would tell his mother that when he grew up, he would take care of her.

She never doubted him and always replied, "I believe you, son."

Where they lived in Georgetown, their neighbor's children would teach Peter what they learned in school. Every day after school at 3:30 p.m., after the neighbor's kids came home, Peter went over to their homes, and they explained what they understood from the teacher the best they could in order for him to learn it too.

I can't remember how long he depended on them, but at the age of fifteen he made money helping foreigners with a little hustling scheme he did at the airport. They loved his attitude and style. When they left the airport, they would keep in contact with him just in case they need help getting around Georgetown. For the time they were in town, he became their tour guide. As the tourists became familiar with him, they felt the need to help him. When Peter informed them about his growing up and that his parents couldn't afford to send him to school, they felt a responsibility to help him. The foreigners tried everything in their power to give him a break to study in the United States. Eventually, the family got his parents to sign his papers and he left with them. How do you think Peter got where he is right now, by sitting back and being mischievous? No, he worked his butt off and studied business in college. Everything worked out for him, and that's how he began to get rich.

I didn't want to leave the first time I visited Peter's home, but the sad part was that I could only be there with Damion and my aunt when Peter wasn't in the country. I loved everything about Peter except his rules. Peter only wanted the people that take care of his home to be there. When he wasn't in the country, Damion and my aunt broke his rules, but he never found out, and it never hurt them. Sometimes while he was there, they would hide me in their bedroom. That's the only place he didn't visit in his home; it was on the second floor among many other bedrooms.

Peter's home was unlike any home I'd ever seen. Everyone in the country called it the Big Mediterranean House because it was three stories high with three verandas, and it was all white with a green roof. Tourists who passed by from the airport would either stop to take pictures, or just to admire it. Peter, his story, and the people he attracted made me interested in the United States of America. I went about the place asking and taking in information on America. In addition to everyone I asked, my grandmother had a very interesting story.

"A couple of months after I had Kimberly," she said, "I went to Canada and spent some time with my older sister, Ariel."

"Where is Canada, Mommy?" I asked.

"It's one of the countries in North America," she replied.

"Damion said that the States is in North America."

"Yeah, the full name is the United States of America," my grandmother agreed. "Canada is after the United States when going north in North America. It's not far from the North Pole."

"It's not too far from where Santa Claus live?" I asked.

"Yeah, he probably lives not too far," she humored me. "My sister wanted me there because when we were small, we got separated," Grandma said. "I didn't see her again until I visited Canada."

"How come y'all was separated?"

"It's wasn't just her. It was all five of us—me, my brother, and my sisters. Elaine is the eldest, followed by Carmella, Ariel, John, and soon after came me, Magnificent."

"You were the last child of your mother?"

"Yep!"

"Just the way I'm your baby, you were your mother's baby?"

"I can't remember spending any time with my mother or father, but there's one thing I never forgot. Some time when I was small, Elaine took us all to a hospital where my mother was diagnosed. She troubled with her throat. If I'm not lying, Elaine said she had large lumps."

"How come she had lumps in her throat?"

"Hold on! Don't jump the gun. I will tell you just now," she said. "I was sitting on the hospital bed at my mother's feet, and Elaine sat with her head, holding her hands and crying. When I asked her why she was crying, she told me not to worry, that everything would be all right. After a while she wiped her eyes, then called Carmella, Ariel, and John to pray. While Elaine prayed, I asked John what was going on, but he didn't respond.

"They were shouting, one after the other, while looking at the ceiling as tears run from their eyes. I was scared and didn't know why they were sad. Soon after they were finished, we all traveled back home. I wanted to ask Elaine why she was crying, but at the same time she looked a little mad. And it wasn't just her; they all looked worried.

"When we reached home, her mood wasn't the same, so I decided to ask her. She said that her mommy was very sick, and that's why she was crying and praying. I asked her if mommy was going to get better, and out of nowhere, tears suddenly burst from her eyes. As she tried to hold it in, the tears kept flowing down her face so she wipe and wipe them away. A few weeks later, we got the news that she died. And after the funeral, we had to move in with different family members. Elaine and John went with some cousin, Carmella and Ariel went to one of their in-laws, and I went with a close aunt and uncle."

"When y'all split up, did you see them a lot?" I asked.

"I saw them every now and then, but after they moved to the United States, we didn't talk until we all became adults. Elaine and John went to Canada, and the in-laws Carmella and Ariel lived with took them to the United States. At the age of fifteen, I left my uncle and aunt's home to live in Georgetown with another relative. My aunt then died a couple months after my uncle."

"Did you get to talk to your brother and sisters during that time since they left?"

"Actually, I didn't hear from them."

Her siblings went off with a greater opportunity, and she was left alone in the struggle. My grandmother wasn't like me. She hardly went to Peter's house; instead, she asked Kimberly to visit. My grandmother was always scared of the Demerara River. I loved the Demerara and the Jet Skis, boats, and the yacht Peter owned. Every time I was going over to Peter's home, my grandmother always told me not to go close to the water because she worried about me drowning. But I never listened. Her words went through one ear and came out the other. Calvin, Damion's younger brother, had taught me how to swim. I told him not to tell her, and he didn't whistle.

While my grandmother and I took a walk around Peter's compound one day, I told her I wanted to be just like Peter when I grew up.

My grandmother said to me, "Never say you want to be just like anyone; always say you want to be greater or better than them. Let's say, for instance, you say you want to become just like Peter. Now, remember you don't know what Peter did or what he went through to become so successful. Always say you want to be better than that person you hold as a role model."

"Damion said Peter studied and took in his education, and that's how he's so successful."

"That's true. He told me the same thing, but he also faced many struggles," said my grandmother. "By saying you want to be greater, whatever struggle or mistake that person encountered, you will not follow, and will perform better. Our thoughts have molding power, and whatever we speak, soon or later, it will come to pass."

Moving forward, I said I will be greater than Peter Joan, but my failing grades were still the same and Ms. Greene still had bad news for my father. Whenever my grandmother got tired of talking to me, she hindered me from going to Peter's house. Sometimes, when she told me to stay home, I would wait until she went and took a nap, and then go over, only to return before she woke. The fifth time I tried to leave when she told me not to, I got beat.

My aunt had asked me to run to the store for her, and by the time I returned, it was too late. While walking up the stairs to enter our home, I remembered closing the back door. She hadn't realized I left, but the door was open.

As I walked up the stairs, the house was silent. It was getting late, and the lights were all off, which gave the impression that she wasn't up. I knew it wasn't a blackout because the neighbor's lights were on. So, I took off my shoes so she wouldn't hear me walk in. Before I could take a few steps into the house, the lights turned on and were quickly followed by some belt lashes. I went to my room crying. A couple of days after that beating, I still went over to Peter's although she said not to go.

CHAPTER 9

In school, Derick and a boy named William got into a fight. William was lying on the floor with Derick on top of him, punching his face. Ms. Greene and Ms. Gloria had tried to break up the fight, but nothing stopped Derick, not even the thought of his mother coming. When William's friends saw him bleeding, they hustled to pull Derick off him, but William took control of the fight. Derick was getting punched, and I was the only friend he had at the time, but I couldn't fight. I only told him brave things about myself to become his soldier. The fight had elevated from wrestling to a fistfight on the school stage. The teachers had disappeared nowhere to be seen. I assumed they went to get the head teacher, so until then it was up to me to stop the fight. William backed up to the edge of the stage, and I went forth and pushed him off, ending it the only way I knew how.

Immediately, the fight was over. He fell on a girl's back, and every living thing went silent. The girl was screaming in pain as students from all corners of the room helped pick her up. In the midst of everything, three male teachers came into the room. One of them grabbed Derick, another grabbed William, and the third grabbed me, and off to the main office we went. That day we became famous throughout the school. As we walked down the hall, students from all sides were saying and screaming good fight.

"Rayfield threw the man off the fucking stage into the girl's back."

Both William and Derick got suspended, and I got punished for three weeks. My punishment was to help the janitor clean the boys' restroom. I would have been suspended with William and Derick, but I had never done anything like it before and my grandmother begged. My grandmother didn't realize the punishment was only one part of the problem. The girl was going through severe pain, because there was a problem with her spine; her mom, who was a nurse, said she couldn't walk. From a distance, I saw it in my grandmother's eyes that she was very disappointed. She grabbed me by my ear and pulled me out the office in tears.

"I'm tired of talking to you. I'm telling you, if you don't stop your nonsense I will send you back to your father. I know I have been saying it for the longest time, and I haven't been doing anything, but keep pushing my but- tons and see what happen."

"I didn't mean to hurt the girl," I said.

"The girl you and the other boys injured have to get an X-ray because of the pain she's feeling. Luckily, her mother is a nurse or Derick's daddy and I would have had to pay for it."

The following day, I saw the girl and her mother in the main office. I was waiting on the janitor, and I apologized for what happened to her daughter's back. The girl said it was okay, but her mother seemed angry. I thought what I did upset my grandmother, grandfather, and the girl's mom. I never liked when my grandmother was disappointed in me because of the struggle my grandparents faced to make sure I had something to eat. For the time that Derick wasn't in school, I acted humble, but when he returned, we were back to square one, or deep in the negatives.

❧✖❧

A month after the incident Derick, myself, and three other friends—Leroy, Tom, and Justin—would get away from school. Three days out of the week for two weeks, we left school after Ms. Finley signed her attendance form at eleven o'clock in the morning. Then, we roamed around Georgetown until three in the afternoon when school ended.

Sometimes, I left them at twelve o'clock and went home to swim in the river with Addie. Damion's older sister was Addie's mom. One of the activities we did while wandering around was seeing who could steal the most stem caps from people's car tires. If we were in a dreadful mood, we would key their cars, or pelt them with bricks and then run off. Sometime we cursed junkies just to irritate them into chasing after us. Although we attended a primary school, the people we encountered thought we were in high school because of the time we were out of school. The color of our school uniform was the same as one of the local secondary schools. Derick did the talking because the rest of us smiled, which made it seem as if we were lying. No matter how dirty our uniforms were for high school students, once Derick said we attended St. John's College on Church Street, they always believed him.

Addie attended Supply Primary School, and we made plans one morning that I would leave school early to meet him at the river. Aunt Kimberly was home during the day, but she hardly came out; Addie said she was scared to be in such a large house. Since Addie was right in Supply, he got to the river earlier and made sure the water was safe to swim in, and that there wasn't any sign of Aunt Kimberly.

Peter had a yacht that was always by the water, and we used to swim around it, pretend to drive it, wash it with the dirty seawater, and push it back and forth.

My aunt wanted me to attend Supply Primary School with Addie, and maybe she was right. It would have saved money on transportation, but I wanted to stick with Derick and the boys. Throughout the two-week getaway event, I only met up with Addie three times; the other times he said he swam with his friends from school. I find it ironic that the day we got caught and carried back to school was the same day Addie got caught too.

There was a restaurant a mile away from St. Angelus called Brenda's Fast Food. Derick cried out for his belly one morning, saying he didn't eat anything before school and that he was hungry. So, we stopped there and decided to buy two small chicken curry dishes for Derick and my-self. Derick lent Leroy some money to buy a large oxtail stew with rice. Tom and Justin said they weren't hungry.

Before the food came, Tom and Justin were eating the salt and pepper that the waitress placed on the table. She told them they can't eat the pepper if they're not buying anything from the restaurant. Both Justin and Tom said they would stop, but Tom didn't.

"Can you please stop eating the pepper? I will ask you to leave," said the girl.

"You can't make us leave. We're customers just like any other customer," said Tom.

The girl went into the kitchen and returned with Ms. Brenda.

"This girl ain't just tell you not to eat that pepper?" asked Ms. Brenda.

Tom and Justin didn't answer Ms. Brenda. Instead, Justin leaned his head over to Tom and mumbled something.

"I can't wait on you fools!" Ms. Brenda shouted. "Get up and leave this place."

A strong, gentle man sitting a couple tables away asked Ms. Brenda if she needed any help getting Tom and Justin to leave.

"Thanks, but I got this," she replied.

"I'm going to kindly ask you one more time to leave this place, or else you will face the consequences."

Tom got up and smacked the pepper shaker off the table. Ms. Brenda bit her lip, grabbed him by his shirt, and pushed him out the restaurant. Justin got up and walked out the door to see what was happening to Tom. I was going to join them, but Derick told me to leave those two clowns alone.

"The woman told them not to eat the fucking pepper, and he's acting like a fucking ass. These clowns love attention. Everybody has to shout at them wherever they go," said Derick.

Some other people in the restaurant were saying how disrespectful Tom and Justin acted. As we were preparing to leave, the windows broke one after the other. Justin and Tom were pelting bricks at the restaurant's windows. When Derick and I ran outside, we saw Tom and Justin hiding behind a car. Tom looked very angry, and Justin said he wanted to go home because he knew he was going to get in trouble.

"What just happened?" asked Derick.

"Tom picks up a few bricks and threw them at Brenda's window," said Justin.

A tall man came out the restaurant with his spoon in his hand and asked, "Who just break the windows?"

Without hesitating, Justin pointed to Tom. The man sprinted over and snatched Tom before he could think about running, then he took off his belt and begin lashing him.

"Loose me! You're not my father!" said Tom.

"Loose the boy or I'll kick you in your face," said Derick.

The man lashed Tom very hard on his back, and Tom went limp, no longer fighting up. The man then beats Tom on his buttocks. Leroy and Justin saw it and ran away, while Derick fought the man to save Tom. The man grabbed Derick by his collar and scolded him. Out of no-where, two men grabbed me by my arms.

"I know which school they go to. I'll take them to the headmistress," said the tall man.

"It's not really these two; it's that one there," said Ms. Brenda.

"I'm going to take all three of them because it's morning, and they supposed to be in school," the tall man replied.

"Okay, thanks," she replied.

He held Tom by his shirt collar and said, "Y'all didn't know I was watching what you were doing every day. The police should pick y'all up."

As we walked in the direction of the school, I kept looking around to see if Justin or Leroy would show up, but they were nowhere to be seen. I remembered begging God not to let my grandmother find out from the headmistress that I was skipping school, but it didn't work. She was crying while talking to the headmistress.

"Adam and I can't put up with this anymore. You need discipline and we're too old. You're taking advantage of us."

Both my mother and my grandma agreed to send me to my father for a short time to be disciplined. I begged her to give me one more chance, but she had made her mind up that I was going with him. As much as my grandfather was disappointed in me, he didn't agree with their decision.

"When you do something wrong, I does try to save you, but you ain't learning nothing. Every other day is something! Nothing good. Something is definitely wrong with you," cried my grandfather.

My mother contacted my father, and it was set that Saturday after work, he was going to pick me up from the market. I cried my eyes out while packing the clothes I was taken to his house.

Aunt Kimberly sat on the bed beside me and said, "See, you don't hear when people talk to you. Now you gotta feel it the hard way."

"Don't cry, Ounga. It's just a month you're going for," said my mother.

Saturday morning came faster than I expected; my grandmother was in her bedroom while my grandfather sat at the table drinking his tea. I took a final look at the cartoon, breathed some of the wonderful air from Supply's atmosphere, and waited for my grandfather.

"Ounga, you're ready?" asked my grandfather.

"Yes, Daddy," I said while staring at everyone with tears in my eyes.

My grandmother got out of the chair she was sitting in to give me a hug and a kiss. Aunt Kimberly tried to beg for me, but my mother said my father was already expecting me. They all give me a kiss, then told me to behave myself.

Since crying couldn't help me, I replied gently to everything, thinking that maybe this was all a trick, that they probably just wanted to make me change. I could tell my grandmother wanted to cry; her face looked unusual. Every now and then the skin by her cheek, eyes, and forehead wrinkled up while she tried to wipe any drop of tears before someone would notice. I told everyone goodbye, except Damion and Calvin; Peter was home so they were too busy.

CHAPTER 10

While my grandfather and I traveled to Georgetown, I was worried and missing them, especially my grandparents.

According to my mother, a month isn't long, I thought. I will behave myself and get to go home before I know it.

"Don't worry, everything will be all right," said my grandfather as he hugged me. "Look how good you were, and now you have to go with your father," he continued, as I bowed my head in shame.

I cried my way to Georgetown, hoping my grandfather felt sorry for me and would call my grandfather when we reach in the market. I asked Robert, but no one had called my grandfather, who left me with Robert to help someone with something. I wanted to go with him, but he had a lot of running around to do, and staying with

Robert was easier for my father to collect me. Soon my father arrived. He and Robert said their hellos, and then he turned to me.

"Hey Junior."

"Hey."

"Where is your grandfather?"

"He left not too long ago to do some work," said Robert.

"Okay, I'm going to take Junior with me. Could you tell him I got him?" asked my father.

"Yeah, no problem," Robert replied.

"And tell him I said thanks for bringing him down for me."

"Okay, I will."

For a few minutes, as we made our way out of the market, he didn't say anything to me, nor did I pay it any mind.

"I heard you've been behaving bad," said my father.

I looked at him without saying a word and continued walking as my heartbeat increased.

"That's bullshit. Your mother and grandmother said you were doing a lot bad things. Just to let you know, you better not try it in my house," he shouted.

I felt as though I was getting the flu. My skin got very hot. I was perspiring and trembling. I thought I was going to faint. I couldn't believe I was going with him to Agricola. Before we hopped on a minibus that would take us to Agricola, there was an important stop he had to make at Kate's sister-in-law Annie's house to buy some fruits. We sat there for a while as Annie and he talked about why I was going to his home.

When he mentioned to her that I love to skip school, she looked at me in a disgusted manner and smiled. Annie husband said my head was so big that a barber would need a map to cut my hair. Then, we left her and headed home.

"Kate, Nathan, and the children are waiting on us, so we can't take long. Just to let you know, we don't live in Agricola any more. Everyone is in Paradise."

"Okay."

"Do you know where is Paradise?" he asked.

"No, Daddy."

"It's up the East Coast. You see how Supply is on the East Bank."

"Yeah."

"Well, the East Coast is the other side," he said.

After forty-five minutes of traveling, we reached the village of Paradise. The streets were numbered and his house was on Fourth Street.

"You see the way your grandparents spoiled you by letting you do what you want. Don't think it will be the same way here."

When we arrived, Nathan, who was Kate's older brother and the father of Amie and Acacia, was home alone.

"Where is them girls?" asked my father.

"They just left to buy something at the store," said Nathan.

"You know Nathan, right?" my daddy asked me.

"No," I replied.

"He was small when I first saw him," Nathan said to my father. Then he turned to me and said, "Hey Ounga, what's up?"

"Nothing much," I replied.

"I heard you've been behaving bad," he said. I stared at him without saying a word. "Wow, man, you looking at me as though you're retarded."

"No," I said quietly.

"Go and put your things in the room," he said while laughing.

Whether I liked it or not, I had to make it home, but only for a month and not any longer.

After a while, Kate and the girls returned. I heard them talking to my father and Nathan in the living room while I was unpacking my clothes.

"Junior is here?" asked Kate.

"Where is he?" asked Emma.

"Junior!" shouted Kate.

"Coming," I said.

"You got big," Kate said, assessing me.

"Yeah."

"Why you're not behaving yourself?" she asked.

I looked at my father as he laughed and said, "I hope he knows what he's doing because I will beat him like a snake."

Nathan also laughed.

"Did you see their children since you came?" Kate asked.

"No."

"They're in the kitchen," she said.

Acacia and Amie were cutting up onions and garlic, while Emma and Erica seasoned the meat and prepared the stew. They all greeted me except Emma, who was upset.

There was a small storage room in the backyard where Nathan and his two daughters slept at night. I went out and sat on the stairs near the storage room and cried for my grandparents, wishing I was home in Supply. As I continued to sit there on the storage patio, I remembered my grandfather saying, "Look how good you were, and now you have to go with your father."

"If only I'd listened to Mommy, I wouldn't have to be here," I cried.

Soon after I gained a headache from crying too much, I went into the bedroom and relaxed. While Nathan and my father sat and argued over a cricket game, Kate and the girls were in her bedroom talking about girl stuff. I went into the girls' bedroom to lie down and ended up falling asleep.

❧✕❧

The next morning when I woke, I was on a mattress on the floor, while Emma and Erica were sleeping on their bed. It was four o'clock in the morning, and everyone was still asleep. The idea to run away and go home crossed my mind, but when I opened the front door, the streets were pitch dark and every now and then something made sounds in the bushes. I locked the door, returned to bed, and forced myself to sleep.

At about six o'clock, Erica woke me up to get ready. I went in the front house and sat in a chair. Not long after I heard my father shouting my name. Before I could get out of the chair, a couple of solid slaps were delivered to me.

"You did hear me calling you?" he shouted.

"I was coming," I cried softly.

"Why you're not preparing for school?"

"I'm waiting on Emma and Erica to finish dressing."

As I sat there while he pounded on me, I felt as if the spirits of Agricola had transported themselves to Paradise. Daddy was right. I was better, but I didn't listen.

There were a couple of phones in the house, but for me to use one would have been taking a chance of life and death. Every day, I was beat severely for taking too long to get ready. There was only one bathroom, and I had to wait until Emma, Erica, Acacia, and Amie had finished bathing. The first and last time I tried to wake early to bathe and get ready before the girls, Uncle Nathan was awake and sent me back to my bed. That same morning, when everyone woke, he told me the pipe water was cold so early in the morning. He knew I used cold water to bathe after the girls were finished. Daddy warmed water on the stove to balance the temperature of the cold pipe water, so their bath wasn't as terrible as mine. Sometimes after a cold bath, my father had me stand in the living room while the back and front doors were open. I would stand there in the living room and shiver from the early morning cold wind that passed throughout the house. I assumed Kate and Nathan couldn't do anything because they sat there and watched him make fun of me.

CHAPTER 11

One morning, when everyone had woken late, I faced the consequences. Kate said Daddy should have woken us up, but he had stayed up late watching the movie 300 with a friend and overslept. Erica and Emma had already finished bathing by the time they woke me, so I would excuse myself and they could get dressed. Daddy was shouting left, right, and center.

"Where is Junior? Is he in the bathroom bathing?"

"He just woke up," said Emma.

"What? Junior, come! Take off your clothes."

I thought I was being sent to the bathroom, but he went for his belt. From the bedroom, he told me to bend and touch my toes. From between my legs, I could see the belt in his hand as he walked out of the bedroom. About two feet from where I was waiting on Daddy, he lashed me on my buttocks with his belt. Erica got scared, Kate cried, and Emma smiled as, one after the other, the lashes came.

After collecting four on my buttocks, I raised my head and begged him, "I can't take it. My buttocks hurts."

Daddy held my shoulder aggressively and pushed my head back down. I was then told if he missed one lash, it would be doubled and severe. My buttocks felt as though it was going to burst. The lashes stung beyond the sting of bees. Soon after he stopped, he made a deal with me. He said either I continue to get beat, which he doesn't mind, or I can use five minutes to get dressed. I chose to get dressed, but after two minutes he returned and lashed me all over my naked skin with the belt. I was screaming and rolling all over the room trying to prevent him from lashing me, but it only made things worse. The harder I made it for him to beat me, the harder he swung the belt at my legs, back, chest, and face.

"Hey Simon! Stop now! He gotta go to school. The more you beat him is more time wasted," said Nathan.

For a moment, my father stared at me mercilessly, his breathing heavy.

"Girls, y'all go. Junior can't come. He'll make y'all late." He turned to me. "Junior, when you're finished getting dressed, come sit in front because I might do something to."

While I was putting on my clothes, my skin burned. I wanted to cry, so the pain would stop, but it only would have made him angry. Before I left the bedroom to go sit in the living room, I heard Nathan and him talking.

"Don't worry with him. He didn't have any intention of going to school from the get go," said my father.

For a couple of seconds, the place went silent.

"What is he doing so long?" Nathan asked.

"Junior! Boy, don't make me have to come back there for you," my father shouted.

I quickly wiped my eyes.

Daddy then said, "Since you didn't want to go to school today, you'll do some schoolwork while you're home."

Beside the front door in the living room was a bookshelf that stood five feet tall and was about two feet in width. There were five shelves that contained small Biblical books, Jehovah's Witnesses Watchtower magazines, and two shelves with the VHS tapes and DVDs they owned.

"Before you start the work your father's going to give you, I need you to count how many books are on those shelves," said Nathan.

After listening to him, I look at my father as he smiled, then walked to the bookshelf.

"Junior, make sure you count all of them right—the biblical books, Watchtower magazines, VHS tapes, and DVDs. If I check them and it's wrong, I will make you count them five times over again, okay?"

"Yes, Uncle Nathan."

I never finished counting those books. Uncle Nathan and my father went over to the neighbors to do something while I was left counting them.

After fifteen minutes, they both returned and asked, "How many books are there?"

"I'm not sure."

"You didn't finish counting how many books is on the shelf?"

"Yeah."

"Tell me how many there are." I said nothing. "What you waiting on, Christmas?" asked Nathan.

"No."

"Then tell me what's taking you so long! Look, Ounga, I done. Your father is going to have deal with you," he shouted then walked out the back door.

"Junior, come!" said my father.

"Yeah," I replied as my heart began to beat fast and faster.

"I want you to study and remember your two times table by the time I get back from work, and you will say it out loud without a book or paper in your hand. Kate will be home to help you. She supposed to be back anytime from the store."

"Okay, Daddy."

Minutes after he left, Kate returned with Crix Crackers and cheese for me to eat.

"I saw Simon on his way to work. He told me he gave you the two times table to study."

"Yeah."

"When you finish with breakfast, take a bath, if you want you can take a nap, then I will help you study your times table."

"Okay, Aunty Kate."

After I had my breakfast, I went into the room and lay on the mattress. I stared at the ceiling while my mind clustered with fear. My entire body got hot, but parts of my body, such as my hands, legs, and arms, were shaking as if I was cold. No matter how much I tried to memorize the two times table, it wasn't staying in my head. I kept thinking about the beating he was going give me if I didn't know it. Unintentionally, I fell asleep. In my sleep, I was in Supply, and it was as dark as midnight with smoke hanging in the air. From the main road, which was quarter of a mile from our house, I heard my grandmother laughing the way she did whenever she was really happy. Both she and my grandfather were happy that I had come back home. I heard my aunt, Damion, and Calvin talking, but I went home instead. I didn't have to knock on the door; when I reached the doorstep, the door opened itself. I was so happy to see my grandparents that I ran to hug my grandfather and started crying.

"Who is you?" my grandfather asked.

"Ounga, Daddy."

"No, you can't be our Ounga. Our Ounga is not coming back," said my grandmother.

"It's me, Mommy and Daddy. I run away from Daddy's house."

"Our Ounga didn't listen when I spoke, so he had to go to his father's where he could be scolded and disciplined," said my grandmother as she began to cry. "If only he had listened when I talked."

I went down to her feet and begged them not to make me go back, swearing that I would behave myself. "Please, Mommy," I cried, but she told me I was already there. I ran to my grandfather and told him I was home. "Please don't make me go back. Daddy will kill me. He beat me on my buttocks."

"Listen to your grandmother," he replied.

I held on to his foot and her dress, and told them I was not going back, and added that I wouldn't lose their clothes. They both began to cry while I bowed my head and screamed. Within seconds, I woke up in my father's house, and Supply was nowhere to be seen. Emma and Erica had already come home and were preparing to study their five times table.

"Do you know your two times table?" asked Erica.

"Not really."

"Make sure you know it when Uncle Simon reach home."

"How you know I have to know the two times table?"

"Mommy told us," said Erica.

"Oh."

"Me and Emma have to study our five times," she said as she walked out the room.

It was getting late, and Daddy was soon to reach home. I couldn't say the two times without looking at the paper. Quickly, I tried to cram as much as possible before Daddy arrived. I went over the times and when I looked at the book, it seemed as though I had it down. But when I closed the book I didn't remember anything. I thought about the dream, of getting beat by Daddy, and I couldn't focus on my two times table. I started talking to myself about how unfair it was.

"Daddy is coming home in ten minutes," said Emma proudly.

"Y'all make sure y'all ready to say the times tables because soon as he gets inside, he will call y'all," said Kate.

"Yes! We ready," said the girls.

"I don't know if Junior is ready," said Emma.

"Where is he?" Kate asked.

"He's in the bedroom," said Erica.

"What's he doing?" asked Kate.

"He was sleeping," said Emma.

"I hope he know the times table Simon told him to study," said Kate as the speed of my heartbeat increased.

"If he don't know it Daddy will beat him like a snake," said Emma while smiling.

"Junior!"

"Coming Aunty Kate."

"Did you study your two times table?" she asked.

"Yeah, I was just studying it," I replied.

"Okay, are you ready for your food?"

"No, not yet." And then I said to myself, "The only thing I want is to try and memorize the other half of my two times, so Daddy won't have to beat me."

As I was about to return to the bedroom, she said, "Sit in one of the chairs with the girls and continue studying because your father will be home soon."

Erica and Emma had the paper with the times table face down on the chair while their eyes were looking to the ceiling mumbling to find out what they remembered. From the kitchen window, Kate had a clear view of anyone passing by before they came into the front yard.

"Simon is coming," Kate shouted.

"Soon," said Emma.

"He's outside."

Both Emma and Erica were happy, they ran outside to greet him.

"Children! Daddy is home," he said as he walked in the back door.

"Junior, are you ready for me?" he asked as I looked at him. "I hope you know your times table because I don't feel I have the strength to beat you right now. But before that, I need to eat some food to get my strength back," he said.

While he sat in the chair opposite mine waiting for his food, he asked Erica and Emma to say theirs three times. Erica went first, then Emma, they both successfully did it and he gave them a high-five saying, "That's my girls."

"Junior! You're next," he shouted.

I got up and went over to him with the book.

"You know you're not using that book to say the tables, right?" he said.

"No, I was using it to study."

"If you revise like I told you to, then you don't have anything to worry about."

I memorized the whole two times table, but when I put the book away and stood in front of him, it vanished from my mind.

"What happened? You don't know it?" asked my father.

"Yeah, but I can't remember it," I replied, fidgeting with my fingers, hoping to recall something.

"I gave you the whole day to memorize just one of the times tables, and you can't even remember half of it. Sad on your side, but I think I'm getting back my strength. What was Junior doing the whole day?" he asked.

"Sleeping," said Emma.

"Oh! You was napping. All right."

"When we came home, he was waking up," said Erica.

"Instead of studying, you choose to sleep. Why, when I tell you to do something, you don't do it, and instead you do the opposite?"

"I was trying to study it, but I fell asleep."

"Well, next time you'll know not to sleep and to do what I tell you." He took off his belt.

"Bend over that chair and touch the stereo," he said, as he folded his leather belt in half holding the buckle and tongue.

Leaning against the wall beside the television was a stereo system. In front of the stereo was a Sausalito oak leaf fabric chair that Nathan loved to sit in. Uncle Nathan placed the chair there because when they watched The Lion King, he loved to have the sound effects loud enough that it was hard for him to hear anything else. Daddy turned the chair sideways in front of the stereo, then told me to lean over the arms and touch the stereo. In order for my hands to touch the stereo, my body would have to hang completely over the two arms of the chair.

"Touch the stereo and don't look back," said my father, as I cried, looking toward the kitchen where Kate was standing.

She had her hands over her mouth while her face wrinkled and tears fell down the gap between her cheek and nose. When I got the first lash with the leather belt, I jumped off the chair arms and rubbed my buttocks, crying and begging him to forgive me.

"Why did you get off the chair?" he shouted.

"It's burning," I cried.

"Next time, you will remember this and do what I said to do."

Emma stood by the front door, smiling.

"If you don't get back on that chair, I will beat you all over your skin."

Without giving me a moment to move, another lash came. Again, I jumped off the chair arms, rubbed my buttocks, and begged him to stop.

"Boy, don't waste my time. I have to sleep. I'm not going to ask you to get back on this chair." He pulled me up from the floor and put me over the chair. Before he could swing the third time, I grabbed the belt. Daddy told me to lose the belt, but I refused. He then started to punch me on my back. I loosed the belt and fell off the chair in pain. Then he punched me in my stomach and told me to get up and get back on the chair.

"My back is hurting," I cried, struggling to raise myself off the floor while he pulled my shirt collar, strangling me.

"Simon! Simon, you have to stop now. You want to kill him," said Kate.

"What the fuck you screaming for? Can't you see he like it? If I give him something to do and he refuses to do it, he have to face the consequences."

"I understand, but you don't have to beat him like that. He has school tomorrow," said Kate.

He didn't respond to what Kate said. Instead, he stared at me, biting his lips and grinding his teeth. The muscles of his jaw flexed, and I stared at him.

"Get up and go to bed, you little dunce," he shouted, disgusted at my presence. I got up, trembling and crying, ready to pee myself out of fear.

"Hurry before I slap you," he said as he bluffed to slap me.

I went and sat on the mattress crying, wishing I was in Supply with Aunt Kimberly and my grandparents. That night I dreamt my grandmother had come to pick me up, but my father told her he didn't want me to leave his house. They got into an argument, and he ground his teeth, making his jaw muscles grow and shrink in size, just like when he wants to kill me. That was the same way he looked at my grandmother. I was going to tell her that I was coming home after school without telling or anyone in his house when Emma woke me.

"I thought Daddy told you not to sleep on our bed?" she said.

"Sorry. Ouch! My back is hurting," I cried.

"Go on the floor where you always sleep."

I quickly crawled off her bed before my father came into the room, and continued to rest. No matter how much I tried, I couldn't return to my dream.

The following morning, I woke up early and bathed before Emma and Erica, but after putting on my clothes, I couldn't find my shoes. I didn't ask anyone if they saw them because they always told my father. I quietly searched the bedrooms and the living room, even Uncle Nathan's room. I searched and searched, but I found nothing. No matter where I looked, I couldn't find them. Eventually, it came time to leave the house, and I no choice but to tell him.

"Junior, what you doing? Why you don't have on your shoes?"

I trembled, not knowing what to say.

"I'm asking you a question. Don't make me come over there and give you a slap," said my father.

"I can't find my shoes."

"You better hurry and find them before the bus reach here," he said while walking into his bedroom.

I continued to search for my shoes, and my father shouted, "You better hurry and find your shoes, or else I'll beat you with my shoes."

As soon as I bent down to look under the chair, my father came up behind me and started lashing me on my back, head, all over my body.

"Where did you put your shoes when you came home?" he asked.

"I left them at the front door," I mumbled, crying.

"No! If you left them at the door, you wouldn't have to look for them this morning. I'm going to ask you one more time, where did you leave the shoes?" he asked, holding his Timberland boot.

"I leave them at the door."

He used his boots to strike me in my head, face, back, arms, stomach, buttocks, legs, and feet. As I tried to protect my face from getting hit, my legs, tummy, and chest were exposed, and he struck as though he wanted to kill me. I cried out to him, hoping he felt sorry for me, but he had no mercy. Hatred was written all over his face.

Suddenly, I was standing next to him and looking down at myself. I wasn't feeling any pain, and the entire house was silent. Ounga was on the floor rolling in pain. Emma was smiling by the bathroom. Kate and Erica were in the kitchen with their faces turned away.

Then, there was an open field with dark grass. The sky was black, and sun reflected a red light through the clouds. In the field, there wasn't anything to fear, but I was running for my life.

A whistle pierced the air, breaking the illusion, and a loud voice shouted, "Get up!"

It was my father, he had stopped lashing, but the leather belt was still folded in his hand.

"Get up!" he shouted, I tried to get on my feet as quick as I could.

"You know you're the only child I have that is a dunce?" said my father.

I stared at him as though he was talking to himself.

"I'm the smartest," said Emma.

"How do you know that?" he asked her, smiling.

"I know," she said.

"Then tell if you know," he insisted.

"When you give me the times tables, I always get them right," she replied.

"Erica always get them correct too, so I guess she's smart the same way," he said.

"But I can say it faster than her."

"It don't matter who could say them faster, once you know them."

"That's why Junior is dunce. He can remember nothing," said Emma.

"His head is big for nothing. Junior, I don't believe you're my child because all my children are smart, and you can't even remember a couple numbers."

I tried to hold in my tears, but sadness got the best of me.

"Why are you crying? I didn't give you anything to cry about," said my father.

"I miss my grandmother."

"You better stop crying and study that times table, because if you don't know them tonight, you will take your pants off and touch the stereo again. So you better start studying while you get the chance."

I left their sight and went in the bedroom. There were belt marks and boot prints across my face, neck, hands, chest, and tummy. I didn't notice any on my legs, but they were hurting.

"Did Junior start studying his times tables?"

"He's in the kitchen. I just gave him something to eat," said Kate.

"Junior, come! Remember what I said I will do if you don't study the tables? I will take your pants off and make you touch the stereo again, while I use all my power to lash you."

I returned to the bedroom to revise the two times while Emma and Erica studied their six times. I went to them and asked for help, but Emma refused to tutor me. She told Erica the tables I was studying were going to confuse them and make them forget what they had to study.

"Go somewhere else and study before I call Daddy

and make him take your clothes off and beat you like a snake. You're not smart like us," said Emma.

"Don't call him."

"Get out the room now before I call him."

"Okay."

"Daddy!" she hollered. "Please talk to Junior!" She laughed as I started to leave, and my father quickly walked into the room.

"What's going on here?" he asked.

"People are trying to study, and Junior keeps making noise," said Emma.

Before I could say anything, my father told me to shut up, then ground his teeth. He snatched me by the back of my neck and pushed me outside. I slipped on the tile and busted my lip open.

"That's what you get when you don't listen. Did you start studying anything?" he asked.

Before I could finish telling him that I was going to ask the girls for help, he began slapping me. "Go outside on the front deck and study that table. When I'm finished with you, you're going to get straight like a nail."

Immediately, I went to the front patio and cried for my grandparents. There was no way I was going to know my two times table. The only thing I thought about was getting beat.

Sometimes, I sat in an old chair my father placed outside and looked out at the bus stop to see if my mother, grandmother, or grandfather had come to carry me home, but no matter how much I hoped, it was always the same thing, no sign of Supply. I had already known what was about to happen. Quickly, I tried to memorize my two times while I watch the clock go nine past an hour. I was perspiring, and my heart beats faster and faster.

"Junior! Come to Daddy."

"God, please don't make Daddy beat me!" I prayed.

"Put away the book and start. You're going first today," he said with a smile.

Emma sat in the chair and held the leather belt. I stood there, staring at him as though he was talking to himself.

"When I sent you to revise, what were you doing?"

Emma had already read his mind. She brought the belt and put it beside him. I tried to show him I wasn't scared or afraid.

No matter what, I will not cry, I thought. I don't care how much he beat me, I can't cry.

But what if he beats you and there's a possibility you can die? You have to cry, said the voice in my head.

Suddenly, I got weak and began shaking.

"If you don't know it, I understand," said my father. "Just let me know, so I can prepare you to touch the stereo."

The rate at which my heart began to beat made my chest hurt. I felt very weak, but my father couldn't have cared less.

"Daddy, please don't beat me," I cried.

"Next time you will know how serious I am when I say revise your work." He looked deep into my eyes and smiled. "Ounga, you know you're the duncest child I have?"

"Yes, Daddy."

He got out of the chair he was sitting in, went over to the stereo, and set the small chair in front of it. "Take of your pants," he said intently.

"I'm sorry, Daddy. Please don't beat me. I will try to remember my two times table if you give me another chance."

"Even if I don't give you another chance, you still have to learn your tables or else more lashes will follow."

"Please," I begged.

"I don't want to hear anything. Take off your pants, and bend and touch the stereo before I start beating you all over your skin."

I slowly took off my pants and walked over to the chair. Kate stood by her bedroom door, peeping. She had her hands over her mouth as tears ran down her face. Emma and Erica got up and went by the dining table.

"Boy hurry up! I don't have time to waste," he shouted.

Before my hand could reach the stereo, he lashed me on my bottom. Immediately, I hopped off the chair, rubbing my buttocks. Emma exploded in laughter.

My father said, "What happened, it bite you? Come back. I ain't done yet."

I can't go back on that chair, my buttocks hurt. I rather take the lashes all over my skin, I thought. Then I said, "I rather die."

"Like you don't understand what I'm fucking saying. Get up."

"Please, Daddy, I will study my two times table," I begged.

"I don't want to hear anything. Get on the chair and touch the stereo."

Again, I stared him as though he was talking to himself. He reached where I was sitting and grabbed me by my collar, then tried to force me to bend over the chair, but for nothing I didn't stay still. He then started slapping on my face and punching me in my stomach. Every now and then I hold my tummy so I didn't feel the full impact of his punches. I screamed for my life and got a few hard slaps on my mouth. I begged Kate to help me, but knew she couldn't risk it. My father got heated and continued thumping and smacking me.

In that moment, I saw myself again and went to the field. I wasn't the only person there this time. Children were running and crying. There wasn't any sun; I only saw clouds of rain.

"Get up! Go bathe your skin."

Jolted from my daydream, I was unaware why he sent me to bathe, but while taking off my pants in the bathroom, I noticed I had peed and defecated myself.

"When your finish bathing come and wipe the pee from the floor," he shouted through the bathroom door.

All I wanted to do was sleep. My chest, tummy, and other parts of my body were bruised and in intense pain. As a result of the welts, I didn't bathe with soap. Even the water burned my skin, but there was nothing I could do other than wash up.

CHAPTER 12

I prayed my father would die when he got a toothache. After work one day, he came home crying about his jaw and his tooth. He told Kate he was hurting something fierce and that the tooth needed to be pulled out. He became very angry at the fact that he couldn't eat the food Kate prepared. No matter what they tried, whether it was providing a stool and cushions for him to place his feet to gain comfort or numbing the gum with Orajel, he continued to whine as a result from the toothache.

I didn't laugh at him, but I stood by the bedroom door peeping at them. I prayed for him to die so I could go home. Eventually, Kate decided he should go to the hospital a couple of villages away. Emma, Erica, and I stayed home with Kasey and Al.

Kasey was older than Al, and Daddy said they were

the best children he had. I used to always get confused between two of them because I mistook Al for a girl and Kasey for a boy. It reached the point where I stopped interacting with them due to fact that my father promised to beat me if I continued to misrepresent their sexes.

After my father and Kate left for the hospital, Erica called me in the living room to relax with them. Erica was sitting with Kasey while Emma had Al. I sat in the opposite chair. After a while Al was getting fidgety; he had a problem staying one place for a while. Instead of letting him run around the house, Emma gave him one of Daddy's tennis balls to play with. He wanted to play catch with Emma, but she wasn't in the mood, so she told me to play with him.

"Y'all go in the hallway and play catch, but just make sure you throw the ball easy to him so he can catch it," said Emma.

Instead of being the older brother and equally sharing the ball with him, I got carried away and played with it alone, which made Emma angry. Every now and then, after I began to play with Al, I had to remind him to throw lightly because the wall lamps could break if I were to miss a catch. For a few minutes, we were having so much fun. Then Al threw the ball onto the kitchen counter where a lamp was sitting.

"What the fuck just happened?" Emma shouted.

"I didn't break it. Al threw the ball into the lamp," I replied.

Emma lashed Al, and then sent him to sit with Kasey and Erica.

"Get the broom and dustpan so we can clean up the glass," said Erica, as she approached.

"Oh shit!" said Emma, displeased.

"What?" Erica looked at Emma.

"Daddy is going to kill Junior when he reach home. The glass broke and fell into the rice bucket."

After cleaning up the glass on the counter, floor, and around the rice bucket, they recite to me how I was going to tell my father the lamp broke and fell into the rice bucket.

"This is what you will say!" said Emma.

"Daddy, when you and Aunty Kate left to go at the hospital, Al was crying so I went into your room and gave him your green ball to play with. He wanted to play with Emma, but she didn't because they were watching the television, so I called him in the hallway to play catch. One time when Al throws the ball, I didn't catch it and it broke the lamp."

Seeing that Emma and Erica had told me what to say, I thought everything was going to be okay. When my father came home after the girls and Al hug and kiss him, I told him what Emma told me to say. After informing him with the news, his countenance changed and he grabbed me by my ears and pulled me into the kitchen where the rice bucket was.

"That's the rice you're talking about?" he asked.

"Yes, Daddy" I replied.

"Oh, cunt, this rice isn't good. Kate! Come and take a look in this rice," he said.

After looking down into it, she told him there were fine pieces of glass all over the top.

"Junior, did you look at it?"

"No, Daddy."

"Take a good look at it," he said.

As I looked at the rice, he asked, "You know what that means?"

"The rice is not good," I replied.

Daddy positioned his nose to the tip of my nose, shouting at the top of his lungs, "Yes! And you know what? I have to dump it. You're going to fucking starve. You're going to fucking starve. Everybody will starve because I'm not buying no more rice."

"I'm sorry for breaking the lamp in the rice."

"Go to your fucking bed before I take off this belt and beat you all over your skin."

While relaxing on the mattress, I thought my grandparents had forgotten me. No one from Supply came or called to find out how I was doing. I cried and prayed to see my grandparents when my father didn't pay attention to me.

When Uncle Nathan and his daughters weren't home, I went into the backyard behind their storeroom and cried until I got a headache. Sometimes when I got angry, I broke the glass bottles my father had around the storeroom into fine pieces and then spread the glass along the fence. Before it got dark, my father use to go outside to take clothes off the line and the jeans off the fence where Kate hung them. I hoped some of the glass would cut his feet when he went to get the clothes. Then, he would die and I could return to Supply. But he was too lucky. It didn't get him, but his friend Dorothy, who was gathering some scrap metal, was cut severely.

Emma and I were salting fish for my father and Kate to sell on the back patio when I heard Ms. Dorothy screamed.

"Oh fuck! Simon, I think something just cut me. I think it's glass," said Ms. Dorothy.

She couldn't take another step, so my father sat her down beside the storeroom in order to bandage her foot before she was able to travel to the hospital. When he took off her shoes, the sock was drenched with blood.

Kate and Erica could not stand the sight of the blood, so they waited on the patio.

"How did the glass get there?" asked my father.

"I don't know," I answered.

"Junior is always playing in the backyard," said Emma.

"Did you break up these bottles?" asked my father.

"No, Daddy."

Hatred and scorn were all over his face. It was in plain sight that he wanted to beat me right then, but because Ms. Dorothy was there, he stayed calm for a while. Soon after wrapping her foot, they put her on a bus. Not long after she left, I got punched and smacked.

"It should have been him. I'm sorry, Ms. Dorothy," I said to myself when I was alone.

CHAPTER 13

T he song "My Neck My Back (Red Red Red)" by Beenie Man got Emma in trouble. It was the first time I saw Daddy beat her. Daddy didn't like the song because there were a lot of profanity and vulgar remarks toward women. Erica told Daddy we heard it on a mini-bus while coming home and that Emma was singing it. He warned us never to play or listen to it again.

But when we were waiting for a bus at the park, a store nearby was playing the song and Emma was bumping and rocking her body to the rhythm. Erica and I didn't remind her about what Daddy said. I stood there and pretended I didn't see her or hear the song. I may as well have covered my ears. After reaching home and as we were doing our homework, Emma started to mumble the song.

"Didn't Simon tell you not to sing that song?" asked Kate.

"I did not sing it," replied Emma.

"So, what did I just hear? I'm sure that's the song your father told y'all not to sing," said Kate.

"I was just humming the rhythm," said Emma.

"I thought Simon told you he don't want to hear anything about the song. Did y'all hear it today?" she asked.

"It was playing at the bus stop today," replied Erica.

Kate didn't ask or say anything else pertaining to the song. When Daddy came home, she mentioned it to him, and everyone was called to attention in the living room.

"Who was singing that song by that singer? What's the singer's name, Junior?" he asked.

"Beenie Man," I replied.

"Which one of y'all was singing Beenie Man's song?" he asked.

"No one was singing it. Emma was humming the song," said Kate.

"Why were you mumbling that song? Didn't I warn you not to sing it?" he asked.

"What was Junior doing?" he asked.

"He was just standing at the bus stop with us," Erica replied.

He told Emma to stretch out her hand, then gave her six lashes with his leather belt. I thanked god I hadn't hummed the song too, because I would have been beaten worse.

Sometimes I was amazed by the way Emma reacted after being beaten. Their relationship only got better. Whenever Emma got lashes, she and Daddy would sit in Daddy's bedroom or the living room and watch one of their favorite movies just a little while after. Sometimes, they were play fighting. I had to watch Emma and relatives that came to visit all play fight with him. He used to tickle and poke them in their ribs with his index finger, which they called the cobra, and the one I wished for, even if it was just once, was being thrown up in the airs.

Erica was probably the only one who couldn't handle Daddy throwing her up. She said it hurt her stomach. Daddy always made Kate, nervous whenever he played with the kids. She said he was rough and wild, and that someone could easily get hurt. It wasn't my place to hate Emma for acting loving toward Daddy because, if by chance, it was my grandparents who had beaten me for something I was told not to do, I would have given them more than just a hug or kiss. But since there was a long distance between us, crying was my only option.

"Can't y'all see Lazarus is crazy? He's always crying and talking to himself," said Nathan.

That soon became my nickname because Uncle Nathan said I had to look like Lazarus from the Bible, who had leprosy, because of the bumps I had on my face, hands, and legs. Only my father's and Emma's beds had mosquito's nets. Even though Uncle Dave never had a net, he and his daughter didn't get bitten by mosquitos as much as I did because of the long bed sheet they used to cover themselves. Times when Uncle Nathan made me look stupid in front of everyone, like when he sent me to count the number of books on the shelves, were a joke for everyone. All I could do was cry and think, I'm going to tell my grandfather.

"Ounga, you're the only dunce child in our family," said my father with a smirk.

CHAPTER 14

I remembered one school morning before I left the house, I was warned not to return home with my school clothes dirty or else I was going to get beat like a snake. During that day, the girls were absent from school, why they weren't going? No one mentioned; I didn't see the value of knowing. If I was to have an award for getting dressed and leaving early, I would have won an Oscar Award that specific morning.

"Junior! Just incase you decide to disobey me and come home with your school dirty or even a button missing from your shirt, I want you to take off your pants, oil your buttocks, bend over the chair and touch the stereo and wait until I reach home Okay."

"Yes Daddy."

During school, there wasn't time to pay attention to what the teacher was teaching, every now and then I'd check to see if any dirt had got on my uniform. At lunch, I stayed in class and ate the food Kate gave to me, and avoided anything that would cause my father to beat the living daylight out of me. My plan was to return home as clean as I was when I left for the house, but there was a problem with the shirt. When school was over and I was putting on my haversack, one of the buttons fell off.

"Oh shit! Daddy is going to beat me when I reach home," I said to myself.

I tried not to cry so the students who stayed after school wouldn't see me as a laughing stock. I went to the headmistress's office and asked her to help me put it on, but she told me there's no way to fix a shirt button without a needle and thread, which she didn't have. I stood there, crying and refusing to leave her office. She then said she could pin it with a safety pin.

"If I go home with my shirt button missing I'm going to get beat," I cried.

"Don't worry, you're not getting beat when you reach home. Just tell your mother or father you was putting on your bag and the button came off, okay?"

"I live with my father and stepmother and he beat me bad."

"Trust me, he will not beat you."

"Okay, Miss," I said even though I knew my father

was going to beat me. I took the headmistress's word to heart and prayed to God while traveling home.

The minute I walked into the house Emma checked me to see what was out of place.

"Aunty Kate, Junior's shirt is missing a button."

"Junior, how did the button come off your shirt?" Kate asked.

"When school ended, I was putting on my bag and the button fall off the shirt," I said.

"Your father will be coming home just now. When he ask you, just make sure you tell him, and don't lie because you know he hates it," said Kate.

"Okay, Aunty Kate."

All over her face I saw how sorry and unhappy she was for me. As I walked toward the bedroom, I overheard Emma telling Erica that I was lying about how the button came off. I was then told to change my clothes and put my uniform in the living room for my father to examine when he arrived. After placing the clothes on the top of his stereo, I reported to the bedroom and pretended to be asleep. Even though the clothes were outside, I believed there was a possibility that if Daddy did not see me, he wouldn't remember to beat me. After a while, as I lay on the mattress, I heard a sound as though someone was knocking the front door.

"It's Daddy," said Emma with a joyful voice

"Daddy, Junior come home with a button off his shirt."

"Where is he?"

"I think he's in the bedroom playing sleep because he don't want to get beat like snake," said Emma.

"Junior!" he called.

I lay there without making a sound or any movement. I couldn't figure out who he was whispering to or what they were discussing, but it wasn't long after that I heard footsteps coming toward the room. At first, I thought he was probably sending Emma, Erica, or Kate to wake me, but I was in for a surprise. Closer and closer the footsteps came, and I felt the vibration of the sound when the door opened. He didn't make a sound or call out for me, just lashed my face with his leather belt. I jumped up and ran to the corner of the room, blocking some of the belt lash.

"Get outside! Get outside and sit your ass down. Don't pretend you're sleeping when I'm calling you. Bare in mind that I will beat you worse, then—I promise—just because you didn't do what I told you."

I quickly ran outside, picked up my uniform, and showed it to him, ready to explain what had happened.

"That's the problem. Why do I always have to beat you for you to do the right thing? You know I'm coming home to check you out, and you're refusing to help me and yourself as well." Daddy looked at my clothes.

"Now, I see you're missing a shirt button. Can you explain to me what happened?"

"Today when school was over, I was putting on my bag and the button fall off onto the floor," I said.

"So you mean to tell me, just like that, the button fall off. You wasn't playing or having anybody pulling your shirt for the button to come off?"

"No, Daddy."

"Okay, Mr. Walker! What you think I should do now?" he asked.

"I don't know, Daddy."

Daddy folded the belt in half and lashed the chair with all of his strength. "Boy, go to your bed and don't let me see you for the night."

I gladly took his offer and did as he requested. Swiftly, I walked inside without looking back while thanking God as tears fell from my eyes. That night, although I had defecated myself, I waited until everyone fell asleep to clean it up.

❧

One day while I was in a corner crying to go home, Kate came into the backyard and caught me. When she asked, I told her my eyes were hurting, but she didn't fall for the lie.

"If you miss your grandmother or grandfather, you don't have to cry. Just tell me and I will see how I can best ask your father to contact them," said Kate.

Kate waited until Daddy came home and told him. I was in the bedroom while they were discussing the matter.

"Junior, come!"

"Were you crying for your grandmother?" he asked.

I looked at Kate and then at him before I answered, "Yes, Daddy."

"Why were you crying for them, because you miss them?" he asked.

"Yes, Daddy."

"You know you didn't have to be feeling this way, but you don't hear, so you have to feel. Go back and do what you were doing. I will call them on the phone tomorrow."

It was more than a week before Daddy actually called my Aunt Kimberly's phone, which gave me the opportunity to speak to my grandmother. Her day couldn't have gotten any better than it was after hearing my voice. During the conversation, she began to cry.

"Kimberly said she's been trying to call your father to talk to you, but she wasn't getting through," said my grandmother.

"I never know," I replied.

"When are you coming home?" asked my grandmother.

I tried not to, but immediately tears fell from my eyes. "I don't know, Mommy."

"Don't cry, son. Baby, don't cry. I will ask your father to send you during the Easter holiday," she said.

"Tell your grandmother you have to get off the phone and that you will call her back tomorrow," said my father.

I told her what he said and then handed the phone to him. While he and my grandmother spoke, I overheard him, saying he was not sending me to Supply because I wasn't memorizing my times table. As they chatted, my father's voice grew louder and louder, almost as if they were getting into an argument. When Daddy got off the phone, he blamed me for the argument that sparked up, which was followed by a thrashing for me.

"You want to go back to Supply, right?" asked my father.

"No, Mommy asked me when I'm coming back home," I replied.

"Don't fucking lie to me," he shouted.

"No, Daddy, I don't want to go back," I cried while he lost his patience.

"What you crying for? You want me to give you something to cry about?" He turned to Emma and said, "Bring my leather belt for me."

"I'm sorry, Daddy. I won't cry anymore."

"Bend and touch the stereo. I'm not going to ask you twice," he said, and tears ran down my face.

I stood there as though I didn't understand what he said. He took three steps to where I was standing, yanked me by my collar, and forced me to bend over the chair. I fought to get off the chair, which eventually made it uncomfortable for him whip me. He then dropped his leather belt and slapped me. I held my face and screamed, kicked, and rolled away.

"Come out from underneath this table," Daddy shouted.

Kate had her hands over her mouth crying, and Erica went outside onto the front patio, while Emma stood there with a smirk on her face, as always.

"Simon, please stop. He's had enough," Kate begged.

"Woman, shut up and go in the bedroom."

"Please, Daddy! My face is hurting," I begged.

"You know it won't be nice if I have to get everyone to help pull you out," he said to me.

Junior, don't go out. Stay under the table, and when he turns his back, run out the back door, said the voice in my head.

When he turned away to show Emma which side of the table to go under so she could scare me in his direction,

I ran in front of her toward the back door. Before I could reach out for the door, a heavy, solid object hit my back.

Then, I was beside him, watching as he beat me with the pointer broom. He picked up the pointer broom and began hitting me with the broom head. After a couple of lashes, he started punching me. I screamed and begged him to stop, but he told me to shut up and continued.

Again, I went to the field. I was crying and running in the rain. While running, I called out for help, but no one heard me. The happy kids were helping each other, and the downcast kids were taking care of themselves. There was a white star, and it seemed as though it was close, but no matter how fast I ran toward it, I couldn't reach it. Out of nowhere I heard:

"Get up! Junior, get up. Don't let me hear your mouth."

"Yes, Daddy."

Only Emma was outside; Kate and Erica were both in their rooms. After a while of having me sit outside, Daddy sent me to the bedroom. Erica gave me some Vaseline to put on the bruises I got from the broom, which made me fall asleep. We hardly ever called Supply. According to Kate, my father wasn't getting through to my aunt, and he called my mother instead. If any of my actions didn't meet my father's expectations, my mother would visit and tell me how to behave, and that I shouldn't make him mad. If only I could have told my grandmother on my mom, then she would have had a taste of how I felt. I wished my parents knew how much I hated them.

The worst time of my life was standing next to my father in the Kingdom Hall. I was burning from the inside out, and so fidgety that I made my own stomach hurt. I wanted to cry and run away; I was still praying for him to die. It was taking too long.

While Kate took the girls out to visit her friend, I was put to torture by staying home with my father. I begged to go, but they said the outing was only for girls. I refused to be in the house alone with Daddy, so I decided to sit outside until they returned. After a while, he came outside well-dressed, and said he was going to one of his friend's place to pick up a movie he wanted everyone to watch.

He hopped on his bike and headed on his way, but not before shouting, "Stay right there! I'm coming back just now!"

I stood by the fence watching as he rode further and further down the road, all the way up until it looked as if he was melting from the heat waves coming off the road. With nothing to do but sit there and wait for someone to show up, I decided to walk around. There were three bicycles beside the house. My first thought was to ride one of them, but I didn't know how, so I sat on the bar and pushed it. The back wheel was flat, but it didn't stop me.

About four houses down, I glanced back and saw someone running up behind me. When I stopped, my father slapped me off the bike, picked me up, and began punching me in my stomach. Then he lashed me with the stick he killed snakes with.

"What the fuck is wrong with you? Can't you see the bike is punctured?" he shouted.

"I'm sorry, Daddy. I just wanted to ride the bike," I cried.

"You like when I get mad, right?"

"No, Daddy. I won't do it again."

Later, I was sent to stand still with my face in the corner of the wall. Every movement would increase how long I had to stand there. After he got tired of seeing me, I was going to be beat like a snake.

A few weeks passed and the Easter holiday approached. I overheard Emma says the two of us were going to Supply and Erica was to visit her father. It wasn't until two weeks before we were to leave that my father told me my grandfather and mother wanted me up there for the Easter holiday, but if I didn't memorize the two times table, only Emma and Erica were going to have a good Easter.

Every free moment that came my way, whether it was on the bus or at home, the girls and Kate helped me to learn. On the day my father planned to have me to recite it, he ended up working overtime, which left Kate as the only adult to make sure I knew it. Kate was way more gentle than my father. She didn't have a leather belt, and she was fine with whatever pace I said. When he came home, they told him I memorized it, but I needed more practice.

"What you're going to do is continue studying when you're in Supply and memorize it for when you come back. Just to let you know, I could make you go to Supply when I think is the right time, but I'll let you go now. Don't feel I can't; I could. Remember, I'm the boss. If I hear you tell your grandmother anything that goes on in this house, I will beat you like a snake whenever you come back, okay?"

"Yes."

"Yes, who?"

"Yes, Daddy."

The following day Erica, Emma, and I woke up early and got ready to leave. Daddy changed the time he went to work because he had to follow Emma and I into Georgetown. Instead of traveling all the to Georgetown with us, Erica took a bus that was heading further up the East Coast to meet her aunt who would take her over a bridge with a car into Berbice. On our way to Supply bus park, we stopped at Annie's stand to collect some banana and mangoes.

My father put them in Emma's bag and said, "Since she's the oldest, she will share it."

But I knew I wasn't getting any. My father didn't understand that the last thing I wanted was something to eat or to see him. The fact that I was going home made me full and happy. Minutes before we reached the bus park, a bus driver called Freaky, who knew my grandfather, saw me from a distance and came running.

"Nobody don't touch him. This is Redman's son. I have to take him home," said Freaky.

"Junior! Who is him?" my father asked.

"A bus driver in Supply."

Freaky overheard, saying, "Don't worry, big boy. I know where he's going. You don't have to worry. He's in good hands." The driver then faced me. "Ounga, where you been? I ain't seen you for a long time."

"I was with my father."

"Okay, okay, so now you're back?" he asked.

I look at my father and said, "Yeah, for Easter."

Before the bus took off, Daddy kissed Emma on her cheek, gave me a tap on my head, and then walked away.

CHAPTER 15

At last! No more Daddy! Supply, I'm coming! I thought.

I looked out the bus window and enjoyed the air, the music, and watched out for landmarks, comparing it to when I last saw it. I had never felt so free. Even if "My Neck My Back" had come on, I would have been bumping to it. It could have been any building or village, but whenever Emma asked about something, I was up and ready to explain who lived there. In time, we approached my village, which looked somewhat different. Either there was more of a view, as a result of the tree being cutting down by the Minister of Agriculture, or people had repainted their houses. Whichever way it was, the Big Mediterranean House was my destination.

"You're on my turf now. Just follow me everywhere I go," I said to Emma.

When I showed Emma where Aunt Kimberly was living, she couldn't believe it.

"Can we go and see Aunty Kimberly before we go by grandmother's?"

As much as I wanted to say yes, I had to say no; Peter's car was in the yard. "Sorry, we can't go. The boss is there."

"Who's the boss?" she asked.

"The owner of the house."

"Who's the owner of the house?"

"Come on. We have to go."

As soon as I walked into the yard, there was my grandmother and Aunt Kimberly doing the washing. I dropped my bags and screamed, running into my grandmother's arms. I squeezed her so tight, not even air itself could separate us. She began crying, which brought tears to my eyes as well. She kissed and squeezed me, squeezed and hugged me until I was breathless. They had only seen Emma couple times since she was born, and they weren't as excited to see her as they were to see me. After a while, I left them and carried the bags to our rooms. Just when I thought it was only going to be my grandparents, Uncle Carlos, and Jimmy for the Easter holiday; there was Carly sleeping in my room. Carly had been Aunt Kimberly's best friend from since their primary school days.

My grandmother always told me to look up to Carly as another aunt, and Carly was also helpful to me as a kid. After lunch, we sat and babbled, making jokes about all things I missed. Before I could open my mouth to say anything, Emma took the mic and said a few things that made me hold my breath.

"How is your father and the family?" asked my grandmother.

"Everyone is good, but Aunt Kate is still lazy," said Emma.

Aunt Kimberly explodes with laughter.

"I'm serious. All she loves to do is sit down in the big chair and tell us what to do. Ask Junior if you think I'm lying," said Emma.

"Is she speaking the truth, Ounga?" asked my grandmother.

"I don't know."

"Look, you trying to give people things to laugh about."

Daddy said not to tell anyone in Supply anything, but Emma is talking and laughing about Kate, I thought.

"You better not let Kate hear what you're saying, or else she might beat you when you go home," said Aunt Kimberly.

"I don't get lashes, only Junior," said Emma.

"For real, Simon does beat him?" asked my grandmother.

"Only when he do wrong things," said Emma.

"Okay."

If only that were true.

Two days before Easter Monday, instead of flying a kite with my grandmother, Uncle Carlos, and Aunt Kimberly, I stayed home with my grandfather and cut bamboo on the land next door. Carly didn't go with the kite flyers, and when my grandfather asked, she insisted on staying home. Carly stood on the back landing and shouted at the top of her lungs into the backyard, asking me to bring up a small bucket of water. There wasn't anything that could have made me angrier than when anything interrupted my grandfather and I from working, especially when dealing with a cutlass. But for the sake of not getting a thrashing from my grandmother, I had to conceal it.

After carrying a large bucket of water upstairs, she spilled it, and then asked me to bring another one. This time, I had to carry it all the way into the house.

"By the time I'm done carrying this water for her, Daddy will be finished cleaning out the wild grass from around the plants," I said quietly.

"Thanks, Ounga. Before you go back with Uncle Adam, I want you to help me fix the bed."

"Which part?" I asked.

"Just now, I will show you," said Carly.

Shortly after taking a bath, Carly came out the bath-room and went into the bedroom. I didn't go in after her because I thought she was going to get dressed first.

"Come inside."

Carly needed help to turn over my mattress. She told me to assist her at the head of the bed while she did the flipping from the foot. While turning over the mattress her towel fall off, exposing her naked body.

"Oh shit, something is wrong with this towel, just hold up the mattress so I can get it," said Carly.

I turned my head away and pretended I didn't see her. She didn't rewrap herself in the towel, she just rested it on a suitcase that stood parallel to the wall behind her. I proceed with fixing the mattress, and then was ready to return to Daddy, but she closed the door and told me to sit down for a while.

"Do you have a girlfriend?" asked Carly.

"No."

"So you mean to tell me there's not a girl you see and like?"

"Not right now."

As Carly spoke, she slowly drifted closer and closer towards the head of the bed until she was looking over me. "What about me? Do you like me?"

"Yeah, Aunty."

"Do you know what this is?" asked Carly.

"My father said it's called a vagina and only girls have it," I replied.

"Do you want to play with my vagina?" she asked.

"No! Daddy is waiting on me downstairs," I replied.

"You don't worry. Uncle Adam is not calling you," Carly yelled.

She pushed her hand into my shorts and started playing with my penis, then smiled and asked how it felt.

"Your fingernail is hurting my birdie," I cried.

She suggested that I take my pants off as I begged her to let me go to my grandfather.

"Just now you will go with Uncle Adam," yelled Carly.

She laid herself out on the bed and opened her legs, saying, "Come and do whatever you want."

I thought, Carly Patacake is very hairy, while I kneeled in the middle of the bed between her legs.

"Just lay down on me, and I will show you what to do," she said.

Carly raised her legs high above my head, and then

told me to make sure my penis was by the hole while she rocked me back and forth. But eventually Carly got tired of my unwillingness and sent me to the living room to watch cartoons.

"Don't let me see you move from there," said Carly, wrapping her towel around her waist. She went out the back door for a while. When she came back with Uncle Carlos, they went up to my room.

At first, I heard Carly saying, "Wait, nah, man."

"Hurry, before somebody comes," said Uncle Carlos.

"Push it back in—harder." She moaned and groaned. "Wait, wait, you lay down and let me go on top of you," said Carly.

The wall that separated my grandparents' and my bedroom had a hole so my grandfather would know when I'd fall asleep to turn my light off. I easily went into their bedroom and peeped through the hole. While Uncle Carlos lay on the bed, Carly was sitting on top of him whining, moving back and forth, and up and down, revealing his penis every now and then.

After a moment, he told her to raise up. I thought he knew I wasn't in the living room, so I quickly returned to watching television. The minute I sat in the chair, Uncle Carlos walked out the room and went into the bathroom.

"Ounga," called Carly.

"Coming, Aunty," I replied.

"Bring a piece of tissue," she said, while I stood at the bedroom door behind the curtain.

"Yes, Aunty Carly."

I stood at the door, pushing my hand behind the curtain so Carly could collect the toilet paper, but she called me in the room. Carly was sitting on the bed, putting her panties and bra back on. I handed the tissue to her and went back outside.

Out on our veranda, looking off toward the southwest where the sun sets, I sat in a plastic chair with my chin on the railing and my eyes half-closed. I wanted to run toward the orange, red, and yellow sunset with all my might and strength, without looking back, but I couldn't. All I could do was sit there and think.

During dinner, I stayed in my grandparents' room trying to erase the images of Carly naked, but there was nothing I could have done to think as a child should. "Come and do what you want." Over and over again, her words invaded my thoughts like a broken record. Supply wasn't as exciting as it should have been. It was supposed to be fun, but things went wrong.

For the remaining days, I stayed in Supply, Carly was mad with me. Why? I wasn't sure, but she tried to get me trouble. Carly told my grandmother I had stared at her while she was changing her clothes in the bedroom. I got in trouble because she was older than me, so no one believed I didn't do it.

The day after Easter Monday, my father called Supply to find out when Emma and I were returning to his house. For once in my life, nothing mattered either way, when horrible things happened. My grandmother told him we would be up there after school the follow day. I wanted to ask my grandmother to let me stay, but I had no control over my feelings. Run away! Run away! Run away without any hindrance! Was what I imagined. Or maybe I could jump into the trench a few houses away from my father's, or not; I wanted to come back home someday.

Bright and early Tuesday morning, we left on our way to school, and then at midday in Paradise. The entire bus ride, Emma was telling Mommy, what she was expecting for her birthday, and my mother sat there agreeing to whatever she desired.

If only they knew how much I hated them. So much anger had built within me that I wanted to scream, but the bus was too full. I sat next to Mommy and bit my lip until it bled. Then, I cried silently and thought, these fucking people don't like me. Supply doesn't like me anymore. I don't know what to do. When I reach Paradise, Daddy will beat me.

I saw my father from a distance; he was waiting on us. The minute we got off the minibus, Daddy was right there.

"Let me check my child just to make sure y'all bring her just the way I sent her," said my father.

"Yeah, you should because when I jump back on a bus to go home, I don't want anyone to call and torment me," my mother replied. "Mommy would love for her son to come back for the summer holiday."

"You heard that. You know what you have to do, right?" said my father, as he looked me in the eye.

"What'd he have to do?"

"I told him for however long he doesn't learn to say his times table without looking at a book, he's not going anywhere."

"One thing I love about you is that you know how to keep him in line," said my mother.

"That shit he try with y'all, he can't try with me."

"Junior is always scared of Daddy. If he doesn't behave himself, Daddy will beat him like a snake," said Emma.

"Just do your job," my mother said and left soon after.

"My son, Ounga from Plounga, how was your vacation in Supply?" asked my father.

"It's was okay," I replied.

"You know, I missed beating you. My hands was itching a couple days ago. When we reach home, we will discuss what went down in Supply, okay, son?"

"Yes, Daddy," I replied.

The sun was blistering hot, and the waves of heat

surrounded me. A beating was on the way. I told myself I didn't want to die, but that if I did die, everything would be okay. I wouldn't be afraid of my father anymore. But I wouldn't see Supply again either. I had to stop thinking because everything led to a bad outcome.

The second we entered the house, he told me to set the bag down at the chair. He kicked off his shoes, and took off his leather belt and put it on his lap.

"Come in front of me, Ounga from Plounga." I stepped forward. "Just to let you know before you talk, I want the truth and nothing but the truth, okay?"

"Yes, Daddy."

"If, by any chance, I find out you're lying, I will oil your whole body and beat you like a snake. You see how I done beat the snake till it died? I will do the same with you. And remember Emma went up there with you, so she will let me know when you're lying. The mic is yours," he said, and I started to shake as my heartbeat spiked and my temperature went through the roof.

Emma told him every second of what Carly had told my grandmother and aunt. She said I was peeping her whenever she was changing her clothes. I had to defend myself to show him that wasn't the case, but instead I wound up telling him what Carly did.

"When Carly told you come and do what you want, what did you do?" asked my father.

"I didn't do anything."

"You're lying. Emma, bring the oil."

I cried and told him that she took off her clothes and pulled me on top of her.

"How you mean she put you on top of her?"

"She opened her legs and put me to kneel down between them." I cried while explaining.

"Did she have on underwear?" he asked.

"No, Daddy."

"Did your penis got hard when you look at her vagina?"

In front of Emma, I bowed my head in shame and answered, "No, Daddy."

"Don't cry. Did your penis get hard?"

"No, Daddy."

"You're sure?"

"Yes Daddy."

"Continue saying what y'all did."

"She raised her feet in the air and then said, 'Make sure your penis is by the hole,' and then she began to rock me backward then forward."

"And what did you do?" he asked.

"I didn't do anything."

"You're lying. You must have did something to make the girl do what she did."

"I didn't do anything. At first I was just with Daddy in the backyard cutting grass."

"And then you went upstairs to peep the girl?" he asked.

"No, Daddy. She asked me to bring water upstairs for her because water don't run upstairs. We always carry it up in buckets."

"And that's when you peep at her?"

"No, Daddy."

"Tell me the truth. I won't beat you. Did you peep the girl?"

"No, Daddy."

"After she rocked you back and forth, what else you did?"

"I was not doing what she wanted, so she sent me out the room to watch TV."

After a while, I was sent to the bedroom, and that was the last time I discussed it with him. I hoped he wouldn't mention it to anyone in Supply, especially my grandmother, and he didn't. But I wasn't sure if he told anyone in his household besides Emma who overheard it all.

CHAPTER 16

Daddy had a Nintendo 64 and couple of cartridges, including the car racing game Top Gear Rally, Super Mario, and Mortal Kombat. I only enjoyed the game whenever Al wanted to play because he always needed help figuring what to do and what not to do. At no time was I brave enough to look my father in the face and ask him to play his games. Not even God could have persuaded my father let me play his games by myself. One night while everyone was sleeping, Al and I were up late playing Top Gear Rally. Due to the fact, there was only one controller, we had to take turns, but it wasn't long after my tenth try that Al fell asleep.

As I was completing the twenty-first level, Emma woke up and said she wanted to play.

"Just now, you will get a chance. I'm gonna win this race," I said.

"Ounga, please pass the controller before I wake up Daddy," she said.

Out of nowhere, Emma grabbed the controller, pulling it completely out of my hands.

"I was playing first, Emma," I broke down.

She quit the level and switched the cartridge to Super Mario. I tried to grab back the controller, but my hand accidentally hit her chest. In a flash, she started screaming loudly.

"What is going on?" my father woke and asked.

"Junior just punched me in my chest, Daddy."

"I did not hit her chest," I replied and he punched me in my face.

"What the fuck is wrong with you, boy? You want me to hit you and show you how it feels?"

"No, Daddy."

"Yeah, man! Stand up!"

"No, Daddy, I'm sorry," I begged.

"I said to fucking stand up."

I got up and my father punched me in my chest.

"Sorry, that was an accident. How did it feel?" he shouted.

"My chest is hurting."

"Good. That's the same way she feel, fool. Now go to your bed."

As I walked away, I heard him trying to make her feel better, and he asked, "Where did he hit you?"

The next day, everyone except Uncle Dave was upset with me. Uncle Dave was never persuaded by the lies Emma told my father or Kate, nor did he ask me the truth; he just knew. A situation had occurred where someone had defecated in the toilet without flushing, which angered my father. The first time I visited, Daddy showed me the bucket we used to carry the water to flush the toilet. If I used the toilet without flushing, he promised to beat me like a snake.

"Everybody, come now! Which one of you mess in the toilet and didn't flush it?" asked my father.

"Daddy, Junior used it," said Emma.

"No! I didn't use the toilet."

"Then who use it?" asked my father.

"I don't know. I was in the bedroom the whole time," I replied.

He walked into his bedroom and returned with his leather belt was wrapped around his hand. "This is the last time I'm going to ask you, who defecated in that toilet?"

"Come on, Junior! If you defecate in the toilet, you don't have to lie. Just say you used the toilet and go flush it," said Kate.

I looked at Kate and then at my father. They were all standing there waiting impatiently for me say, "I did it."

"Come on, Simon. Spare him this time. Just let him get the water and flush it," Kate begged.

"I'm not beating him because he didn't flush. I'm beating him because he's lying."

"That girl is a liar. The boy didn't mess in the toilet. She's lying on Ounga," Uncle Dave said.

"What?" asked Daddy.

"Emma is lying on Ounga," said Uncle Dave.

"How you know she's lying?" asked my father.

"Trust me! She's lying on Ounga. He didn't leave that room to go into that toilet!" Dave shouted.

"But he just said he used the toilet."

"Ounga, speak the truth. Did you use the toilet?" asked Uncle Dave.

"No, Uncle Dave."

"No, he only said that because you're representing him," said my father.

"The boy is scared because the belt's in your hand. He'd say anything you want to hear."

"He's my son, and I can beat him if I want to," my father shouted.

"Okay," said Uncle Dave, and he returned to the bedroom.

"This is what I want you to do now," Daddy said to me. "I'm going to fix the chair at the stereo and you're going to take off your pants without making a sound. Then, you're going to touch the stereo for me, okay?"

"Yes, Daddy."

I wished Daddy would die. I wished he wasn't my father.

"I'm gonna learn my times tables properly, go home, and never come back here ever again!" I cried before Daddy made me take off my clothes and underwear, and then beat me on my buttocks.

I feared him too much. All I could think about were the beatings he loved to give me. I could not retain the tables the way my father wanted. As a result of the beatings being so painful, I found it better to focus on death. I told myself that one day, he would beat me until I died. I began to hope that today was that day. I talked to myself in my mind, asking my grandmother to forgive me for wanting to die without seeing them again. She told me long ago that when you die you go to heaven. My grandmother said when she dies, she will be going there. So, after I die by Daddy's hand, I will see my grandmother.

"Don't look at me. Bend over and touch the stereo," said my father as I trembled after taking off my clothes.

That time I didn't worry about what was going to happen to my buttocks. I kept my head down and looked at the floor in front the stereo, letting him freely act the way he loved to treat me. Someone slammed a door while Kate cried, her nose sniffing every now and then. With all his might, one after the other, Daddy shouted out like a Spartan warrior before he lashed me on my buttocks. After the seventh lash, I couldn't feel my buttocks, as if the nerves weren't functioning. Like they had died. My father said my buttocks had gone blue, as he drenched himself in sweat. As much as wanted to cry, I didn't. Only death was acceptable.

CHAPTER 17

I choose a day when Emma and Erica stayed home from school. Immediately after school let out, I traveled to the market to look for my grandfather. When I saw him, tears filled my eyes and ran down my cheeks.

"Daddy! Daddy!" I cried from a distance.

"Ounga?" he replied.

"I can't go back. Daddy will beat me."

My grandfather welcomed me into his arms with a bear hug and a kiss on my forehead.

"You're coming home today?" he asked.

"Daddy said I can't come because I don't know the times table properly, but I can't go back because he will beat me."

"Don't cry. You don't know the times table?"

"I do, but Daddy's scary when he holds the belt."

"What time you expected home?" he asked.

"I don't have a special time to be home. All they told me was as soon as school's over to come home."

"When I reach home, I will talk to your grandmother, okay? Don't cry. You will come back home, okay?" As much as he didn't want to send me back, there was nothing else to do.

Before leaving the market, my grandfather handed me a hundred dollar bill and said, "It is your own, don't let them see it."

"Okay, Daddy."

"Bye bye, Ounga," he shouted from a distance.

Seeing my grandfather and knowing he would talk to my grandmother made me feel lighter. In a vision, I saw myself excited at Peter's home, preparing to take a ride on one of his Jet Skis. This is what you're missing. Let's go up to Supply, said someone in my mind.

Approximately two weeks after I visited my grandfather, he told me he talked with my grandmother and they agreed I would be allowed to spend one week with them.

That was all I needed.

The next day, the second I reached home, Emma was making jokes about how Daddy was going to beat me when he arrived. I didn't pay her any mind because she always made me a laughing stock, whether I was supposed to get beat or not. Similar to any other day after school, I did my homework, hung up my uniform in the closet for the next day, and then stayed in the bedroom far away from everyone else.

I fell asleep, and Daddy woke me up by beating me with a pointer broom. As I screamed, he lashed all over my body and questioned me about telling my grandmother what was going on in Paradise.

I cried, "I don't know!"

He slammed the door shut before I could run out and continued lashing me.

My head, eyes, and lips were bruised and swollen. My stomach was upset from the punches. I couldn't walk because he had stomped on my toes, heel, ankle, calf, shin, knee, thigh, and waist with his Timberland boots. After he sent me to bathe, I realized I'd peed and defecated myself. Emma called me Shitta Batty.

I couldn't recite my times table, but he decided to send me to Supply for a week anyway. Friday morning, as the girls and I was leaving my father's house, he reminded me that if I mentioned anything to my grandparents, I would be beaten like a snake. On our way to school, Emma teased me about the beating Daddy promised me when I returned. Because I didn't have to travel home with Emma and Erica, I didn't mind of seeing or being in their presence. As the clock struck three and Ms. Stacy dismissed the class, I ran outside and was on my way to Stabroek Market to meet my grandfather.

"There is no way Emma and Erica are going to stop me from going home today."

"You wanna wait on me, or you wanna go home?" asked my grandfather when I reached the market.

"No, Daddy, I will wait on you."

I sat my book bag in my grandfather's stand and went to visit his daughter Eva, who was a market vendor. For a living, Eva sold leafy vegetables and managed her husband's store in Parika, where they lived. After a while standing there and assisting Eva by spraying water on her vegetables while she bargained with customer, I earned some money to buy candy. Aunt Eva wasn't my grandmother's daughter; she was the daughter of my grandfather's first wife. Aunt Eva and her brother visited us on the holidays. My grandmother never got along with Aunt Eva, but for the sake my grandfather, my grandmother tries to overlook their problem.

My grandmother said the problem had occurred around the time she was pregnant with Aunt Kimberly. Eva had kicked her in the stomach because she was jealous of my grandfather having a second girl. I asked my grandfather, and he told me it was true, but he said it was something that was a long gone problem.

On our way home, I used the money I got from Eva to purchase a few snacks and candy, which kept me satisfied during the bus ride. Supply had not changed while I was away, and Carly was still around. My grandmother wasn't home from work yet, but she had cooked food and left it for us. Egg curry for me, and salt fish with Dal and rice for everyone else. While sitting at the dining table, the thoughts of what I should and should not tell my grandmother came to mind. For the couple of hours until my grandmother came home, I refreshed my mind on what took place in Paradise and prepared to talk.

Sometimes for breakfast at my father's home, Erica and Emma would make a special soft bake they called monkey ears. I remembered making some to show her how much I appreciated her letting me come home. I made some for my grandfather, but he said it was too oily.

Not in a million years would I ever have thought my grandmother would have gotten so angry when I told her that my father beat me whenever he felt like it. While speaking to the officer, my grandmother cried as indecent language forces its way out of her mouth every now and then. Soon after, Kimberly and Carly came over, breathing as though they had run a marathon.

"Is that what happened, Daddy?" Aunt Kimberly asked my grandfather curiously.

"Every fucking time the boy go there, his daddy always beating, beating, beating him. For what? He look like a punching bag?" said my grandfather annoyed.

"No! Simon will not beat him again. Saturday we're going to see the probation officer," said my grandmother.

The probation officer? I thought, and then said, "No, we can't go. He'll beat me."

"Quiet. Tomorrow we are going to the probation court and you will tell them everything Simon did to you."

"Okay, Mommy."

"Where's the probation officer, Mommy?" I asked.

"At the probation court. You're going to be with one of the probation officers in a room with your father, and you're going to tell the officer what he did to you."

The days of the week came and went, but Saturday took its time as we gathered at the court. My dad's mother, Margarita, better known as The Chimney, his sister Patty, Kate, Erica, and Emma had come with him, but he was nowhere to be seen. Soon after, an officer appeared and took my mother and grandmother into a room. The officer returned and instructed the rest of us to have a seat in the hallway. Kate and Erica were the only ones who greeted me, the others looked disappointed. Margarita put her head out the window to exhale her cigarette smoke.

A little while later, they all came out the room with the probation officer. My father hugged my mother and grandmother, and embraced Margarita as we walked out of the building.

"I think the decision is right," said my mother.

"What did the probation officer say?" asked Margarita.

"They will take turns. One weekend Emma will come to Supply and the other weekend Ounga will go," said my grandmother.

Immediately, I got scared and quietly asked my grandmother if I had to go see my father.

"Not now, the following week," Mommy responded.

For the second time, they all hugged each other, and my grandmother and I left and went to the market my grandfather worked on to shop for groceries.

The following Saturday around two in the afternoon, Emma and my younger sister Lina showed up with my mother. Nothing else in the universe could have made Aunt Kimberly and my grandmother happier. But I didn't really want to approach Emma or my mother, so I said hi to them, and then escorted Lina to my room where the girls had to sleep for their time being there. As I kept Lina company while she unpacked her haversack, she started to cry. At first Lina didn't want to talk about what was troubling her, but Lina said she wanted to go home.

"Don't worry. Isn't it tomorrow y'all leaving?" I asked.

"I don't know. Mommy never told us when we are going home."

After a while, I got tired, left her with her things, and returned to my grandparent's bedroom. Her reaction reminded me of the way I used to cry at my father's house to come home.

"But it's not like someone is beating her! Daddy was beating me. That's why I was crying to come home. I had to miss my grandparents too," I said aloud to myself.

Later that night, everyone except my grandfather and I sat in the living room and went over how the visits Emma and I had to make back and forth between my grandparents and my father affected us all.

The following weekend, it was my turn. Kate collected me from my grandfather's when she stopped by the market to change some money her mom brought back from the United States. Kate greeted me with a smile and a hug, but I was confused as to why she acted so nice. A few weeks earlier, I was nearly the cause of my father ending up in jail. While traveling on the bus, Kate suggested we stop at Daddy's workplace to surprise him. I wished she had told me I couldn't come that weekend, and to return to my grandfather. My father and couple friends from the Jehovah's Witnesses' meeting he attended were rebuilding someone's house.

Surprisingly, the second we stepped into the compound, my father shouted, "Hey son, what's up?"

I didn't reply. Instead, I stared at him as though he was crazy.

"Come pass me couple nails from the bucket over there," said my father in a friendly manner.

I did what he requested, then returned to my seat as if I was still under his old control. Roughly twenty-five feet from where I was sitting, Kate was conversing with my father. What they were talking about I couldn't figure out, but I know it was pertained to me. As a steady stream of words flew out their mouths, Kate kept looking over in my direction. When she asked me if I wanted to stay and come home with my father or leave with her, I refused the privilege of leaving with Kate and overlooked my fear.

"Yeah! I will stay with Daddy."

"Okay, then I will see y'all when y'all come home," said Kate and then took off.

"Junior! Come. You don't have to be over there. You can sit right here and watch me work," my father yelled from the ladder he was sitting on.

Softly, I replied, "Okay," but if he only knew how uncomfortable I felt in his presence.

"When you become a man," my father said, "you might end up doing this same work. So watch and learn."

If he had only known the last thing I wanted was to be there with him. If only it was my grandfather working; I would rather be with him.

As the day turned to the night, my father and his friend decided they would stop working and leave whatever was left for the next day. While they were changing their clothes, one of his friends, Carlito, who attended their Jehovah's Witnesses meeting commented to everyone that I was a lot quiet than my father and his other children.

"He doesn't live with me. He lives with his grandparents," said my father.

"Okay, okay," they all replied.

He had mentioned to me that we were only a few miles away from home, and we were going to walk the distance. I grabbed my backpack with a couple of briefs, my toothbrush, toothpaste, and toilet paper, and put it on my back. My father tried to make a joke, asking me if I was going to carry his bag, but I didn't feel comfortable making any jokes.

After walking for about ten minutes, not another word came out of my father's mouth. Only the creatures, people, and things in the village were active. Frogs in the dark bushes made weird sounds. The street lights steadily blinked as though someone was tampering with the electricity. Folks went about doing their last minute duties before they closed up and prepared for bed. The mosquitoes tormented us as we walked down the road. Even the fish in the trench splashed; I wondered if they were fighting for their last meal or in the process of their father beating them.

"Did I treat you badly when you were staying with me?"

My entire body and mind went paralyzed, just for a few seconds.

"Come on, tell me! Don't be afraid," he said, raising the tone of his voice.

"No, Daddy."

"So, why you went and tell your grandmother, I beat you? If I was treating you bad, you should have let me know."

Again, I went paralyzed at his question. He didn't know? I thought curiously.

"I want us to forget about what happened and be a father and son to each other, okay?"

"Yeah, Daddy."

That was the last conversation we had before they made me appreciate Kate even more than the times she saved me in Agricola. When we arrived, everyone except Nathan and his two daughters were in the kitchen cooking.

"Whatever that is, I was smelling it on the road," my father yelled across the house.

"They're punishing us. The food smells good, but it's taking too long to finish cooking," said Nathan.

While Daddy went and discussed the cricket game with Nathan, I went into the bedroom, put up my bags, and then changed my clothes. That time I visited was the first time I met Kate's mom, Catherine. On our way to school Monday morning, Emma and Erica told me Catherine came from the United States of America and that she was taking them back with her.

"While you have to go to school in Guyana and get beaten by the teachers, we will be in America having fun," said Emma.

"You wanna know what I'm gonna enjoy the most?" asked Erica.

"What! Don't tell me, the plane," said Emma.

"How you know so well?" said Erica joyfully.

The following weekend, Emma didn't come to visit, and I couldn't have felt happier. Instead, I received an invitation to attend Kate and my father's wedding. I explained to Aunt Kimberly and my grandmother that going to my father's wedding was the last thing I wanted to do, but they forced me.

"All of them hate me. When we were at the probation court, they didn't say hi to me, and Daddy's mother was mad at me," I cried, trying to persuade them.

"You don't have to worry about them. You're just going for the food and anything Kate's mom might have brought for you from the States," said Aunt Kimberly, smiling like the Grinch.

The minute my mother showed up, there was nothing I could have said to talk my way out of it. My mother had come to bring me to the wedding and was supposed to take me home after the wedding. Instead, she left me in Paradise with my father and his family on his wedding night and proceeded with her own life. There wasn't a phone, and I wasn't going to talk to anyone I wasn't familiar with or who didn't like me. I was stuck all alone, cursing my mother for setting me up. After leaving the church, we headed to the hall, which was about a mile away from my father's house. Once at the hall, all I needed was for someone to take me to the house. Since ninety percent of the things Catherine had to say about me were good, which I hadn't expected, she was my target.

Catherine said she knew me when I used to visit my father in Agricola. Kate told her over the phone on how well Faith and I get along. Catherine collected Kate's keys and walked me over to the house, made sure I was okay, and that I had something to eat until they all came home from the hall. I made sure she was far away, locked the door, went into the bedroom, and cried myself to sleep.

Early the following morning, Emma woke me up telling everyone except the adults were going to Guyhoc

Park to spend the day with my father's dad, Michael, and Margarita. My father's house was full of his relatives and some of Kate's, who came to welcome Catherine back after being in the States for a long time. Just as I was about to take a shower, my father said that by the time I'd finish everyone should be ready to leave. The next thing I had to do was get dressed.

"Just wash your face and get the boogers out your eyes," said Kate.

Patty's two sons, Alton and Aston, were the right deal. They couldn't have cared less about washing their face or cleaning their teeth. The second they woke and found out what my father and Kate had planned for the day, they got up, got dressed, and were waiting in the living for everyone else with boogers in their eyes and bridle from the corner of their mouth to the bottom of their ears. My father had said to them and in front of everyone, that it was only me he expected to do something like that, and everyone laughed. After Alton and Aston were sent to clean their faces, we were all off to Margarita's house. As we traveled on the bus, Alton was informing Emma and Erica what to expect at Guyhoc Park as things had changed since the last time they visited.

"When we reach the park, we'll ask Aunty Patty to go in the Blacka," said Emma.

"You mad! Nought people died in the Blacka," said Aston.

"Not all the time, only when it's high tide. Even the people who swim there said when the water get high, something does come up and pull you down," said Alton.

"It wouldn't have to be high tide for Junior to drown, his big head will pull him down," said Emma, while everyone burst out in laughter.

From that moment, Emma started telling them about the way my father had beaten me, which became the joke until we reached Guyhoc Park. There were all new faces, except Margarita, who lived upstairs, and Patty, who lived downstairs. They said Michael was going to be there, but everywhere I looked, he was nowhere to be seen. Every now and again as I was acquainted to their relatives, they kept saying I was the spitting image of Simon and the younger version of Michael, which I didn't appreciate.

All of a sudden Alton and Aston begin shouting, "Grandfather, come home!" and storming up all the children to run out and gather around him.

They didn't tell me he was living in another country. Michael came in a taxi with two large suitcases and a backpack on his back that Aston and Alton fought to carry. As I slowly walked down the stairs and approached the front of the park where they all were, from Emma the eldest to Aston the youngest, all the kids were asking Michael what he brought back from Barbados for them.

I sat on the front porch beside Patty, and after a while, he came over hug and kiss her. Then, he asked, "Who is this? Ounga?"

Before I thought about giving him a hug, he rubbed my head and asked how I was doing.

"Fine, thank you, grandfather."

It sounded weird to call him grandfather. He looked just like my father, and I couldn't stand it. All he did was rub my head; didn't even shake my hand or give me a hug. I didn't get anything from him, not even a candy; he gave the kids goodies and some money, and went away for the day. Later that afternoon when my mother came for me, he wasn't anywhere to be seen, and we had to leave.

When we arrived in Supply, I saw a boy in Peter's yard helping Calvin wash Peter's green SUV. I tried to call out to them, but for some reason they didn't hear me. I later found out that the strange boy I saw, Addy, is related to Damion and Calvin. I didn't get to meet Addy until I came home from school the following day. After exchanging names and hobbies, I questioned him to find out how where he came from, how long he came to stay, and if Peter knew him.

"No! I don't know Peter. If he sees me, Uncle Damion and Calvin will get in trouble," said Addy.

"You ever see Peter?" I asked.

"Yeah! For the whole weekend," Addy said. "Uncle Damion put me in the closet the minute he stepped out the house to assist Peter, and I came out and peeped through the window without them seeing me."

"You weren't scared if they see you?"

"No! You barely pull the blind, making sure they outside and can't see in," he said.

"So you'll be living with Damion and Aunty Kimberly?" I asked.

"Yeah, if you want you can stay over, and I'll show you how to pull the blind," he said.

"I can't stay over late. Tomorrow, I have to go to school."

"Can you stay home tomorrow?"

"Mommy don't like it when I stay home from school," I said.

"You live with your mother? I thought you lived with your grandmother and grandfather."

"Yeah, I live with my grandmother and grandfather. I call them Mommy and Daddy because I grow up with them since I was a baby, so they're the parents I know.

"Where do your mother live?"

"She lived over the river with her boyfriend."

"Where over the river she lives?"

"Where over the river she lives?"

"I don't know."

"So, you call your grandmother, Mommy? I call my grandmother Granny and my mother Mommy."

"Where is your mother?" I asked.

"She is in the hospital for using drugs. That's why I'm here with my uncles, but she's coming out soon."

"Where is your father?" I asked.

"I don't know. I never had the chance to meet him."

"Where is your father?" he asked.

"In Paradise, I don't like him."

"Why?"

"I don't what to talk about it."

While Peter was in the country, I pretended not to feel well, thinking I would have stayed with Addy and my aunt. Unfortunately, Carlos and his friend Leighton were home. It was ten in the morning, and I was laying down in my grandparents' bed while they were in the living room. Since I had to stay home with my uncle, I decided to watch some cartoons. I asked my uncle to call Addy, but he refused; he wasn't in the mood to do me a favor. After a while, I looked for Uncle Carlos, but he was nowhere to be seen. I assumed he felt sorry for me and went to get Addy to stay with me. Never having gone wrong with

Channel 28, I turned it on. From ten to eleven-thirty, it showed Spongebob Squarepants, and from eleven-thirty straight through to one-thirty, it showed Tom and Jerry. As I'm sitting there watching and smiling every now and again, Leighton emerged, smiling, and set up the DVD player.

"Just now, I will turn on back your cartoon, I just need to watch this thing, okay, squady?" said Leighton.

"Hurry up, the cartoon will be done soon," I said annoyed.

"Don't worry, you'll love this," he said, smiling as he walked toward the chair behind the one I was sitting in.

It was a porn DVD he played. As the woman in the film took off her clothes and underwear and began to suck the man's penis, Leighton took off his pants and his shorts. He lay back naked in the chair with his legs open and his penis in the palm of his hand, pumping it back and forth.

"Hey! You can't watch this blues with clothes on," said Leighton.

As I got up and began to head for my grandparent's room, he stopped me.

"Take off your clothes, and do what I'm doing," he said.

"I can't."

"Bana, you don't hear?"

"Okay, Leighton," I cried.

While I sat in the chair and did what he asked of me, tears forced their way out of my eyes, but I quickly slanted my body away and wiped the tears away so he didn't see them. For a few minutes, I wondered if he didn't care about anyone entering the house; whether it was my grandparents or Uncle Carlos. Leighton added a little more volume to the television when the woman has the man inserted his penis into her vagina and told her to take it; then he asked me to come over to his chair where he told me how to pump his penis. Leighton was getting angry as a result of me not doing it right. He shouted, telling me I had hold it tighter and pump it faster.

From that moment, I thought Leighton and Carly were the same because after a while he got up turned off the television and told me to go in the bedroom. Leighton lay on the bed and told me to do whatever I wanted with him. I couldn't. I stood there in shock, watching him. I didn't know what to do. My penis didn't get hard even when he tried to play with it.

"Lay down and let me show you how you supposed to it."

"I can't, Uncle Leighton."

"Why?" he asked. I stared him as though he was crazy, but said nothing. "Just lay down and relax."

Then he came closer to me. "Come on, Ounga. Relax your buttocks."

"It's hurting," I cried.

As I laid there crying, Leighton told me to calm down. He wasn't going to take long. As I lay there, memories from the time Bryan, Casper, and Carly touched me came all at the same time, and then what was happening with Leighton. Then, I went to the field. There was a reasonable number of kids as well as myself. We were all sitting and crying. I begged them to run away with me, but they said they were tired and scared and couldn't do anything to help.

I cried, while begging them not to cry. All our laughter was demolished by wickedness.

Leighton got up and told me it was my turn.

"Put your penis inside." I ran out the room and started crying. "I can't, Uncle Leighton.

"You don't have to do it. You can watch your cartoon."

"I don't want to watch cartoons anymore."

"Don't tell nobody."

Angry at everyone and everything, I stayed in the backyard and waited until it got dark before I went upstairs when it was time to sleep. I stopped crying because it made me feel helpless, as though someone was supposed to feel sorry for me, when I couldn't even tell them and they didn't even notice. That night, I laid on the same bed, my bed, just a few inches away from where I was troubled. I looked out at the dark sky, moon, and the stars, and wondered what was going on beyond what my eyes could see.

"Maybe other people are in space. Maybe aliens are flying around, making sure their children are okay."

CHAPTER 18

I got in trouble for wearing my grandfather's briefs. Every Saturday when my grandmother was going grocery shopping, she had to buy me a pack of briefs because after I wore them, it was impossible to know where they went.

"When he pees his pants, instead of washing them, he throws them away," said Carlos, after my grandmother confronted me.

She probably believed he was lying, but I didn't deny it in front of him. When asked by my grandfather, I told him I didn't urinate in my briefs or throw them away. My grandfather probably thought about what Carlos said, but it didn't matter; he never beat me. I was his last baby, as he told everyone he knew. The only thing I was sure of doing was wearing my grandfather's brief when I couldn't find mine. After a while, my grandfather started hiding his briefs, which meant I had to travel around briefless. One of our neighbors, Charlie, owned a mango tree that everyone went crazy for, which leaned over into our yard. One afternoon, Addy and I had decided to ask Charlie's permission to climb his tree and pick some mangoes. Since Addy is an expert at climbing, his job was to go up and shake the tree limb to the best of his ability while I gathered whatever fell. As I waited for him to rain mangos, I had to urinate. I went to the corner of Charlie's fence, and while zipping up my pants, my penis got caught in the zip. I screamed at the top of my lungs, standing by the fence holding my penis, shaking with shock. It felt as if my skin was being torn when I tried to unzip it. My grandfather and Uncle Carlos came running into Charlie's backyard to carry me home.

When my grandfather tried to see what happened, my penis was bleeding.

"In order for his penis to be unzipped, I will have to zip it down," said my grandfather.

"Then do it. What you waiting for? He doesn't listen. I told him to care his briefs, and now he don't have any to wear," said my grandmother.

It took us a long time before we could untangle my penis from the zip because I was crying and behaving crazy about losing my penis. My grandmother was joking when she said there was a possibility I would lose my penis and turn into a woman. I calmed down when I heard Calvin was going to ride Peter's Jet Ski later that day. They tricked me. They told me in order for me to get over there to ride the Jet Ski, I would have to walk, which I wasn't able to do with a zipped up penis. So I let my grandfather do it.

The Common Entrance Exam was approaching, and I needed help in school to prepare for it. Aunt Kimberly told my grandmother, I had to do well in order to attend a good secondary school. When my mother heard about the exam, she decided that I needed to stay with her where I could attend Ms. Jones's after school lessons. My mother's child's father, Mark, was related to Ms. Jones. Mark's older brother, Mitt, had two kids with Ms. Jones's daughter, Latoya. Mark and my mother lived over the river with his mother in a village called Port Rime. The second I arrived there, everything seemed nice because Mark had a shop. His father, Mr. Bone, owned a car and their house was somewhat okay. There was a standpipe in the Bones's yard; in Supply, my grandfather and I had to fetch water from our neighbor, which was about half a mile away from where we lived.

Mr. and Ms. Bone lived upstairs with their two other sons, and Mommy, Mark, and their daughter Akhila lived downstairs. There was something about me that Mark couldn't stand. When he arrived in the house and saw me in the living room watching cartoons, his mood changed immediately. I greeted him, but he didn't reply politely. Mark kissed his teeth, then walked into their bedroom.

"What he's doing here?" Mark asked my mother.

I was surprised he said it loud enough for me to hear.

"Remember I told you he's soon to attend high school; he has the common entrance exam coming up, so I think we should send him to Ms. Jones," my mother replied.

Again he kissed his teeth, but at her that time.

I remembered thinking how small and dirty their house was. Mark always had something bad to say about me, but he failed to evaluate his own surroundings.

"Where you going to sleep?" Mark asked me.

"Mommy said I can sleep in the chair," I said.

"Nobody is allowed to sleep in the chair. You will have to sleep on the floor."

"Mark, he can't sleep in the chair?" my mother asked.

"No!" he shouted.

When he or my mother went to Supply, I would have had either had to give up my bed or they would have had the couch to sleep on. But I had no choice except to do what he said, and every other minute a baby or a giant ditch frog would jump beside me.

After school when I arrived at Ms. Jones's lesson, it

surprised me that I was the only student she had. On the other hand, she was amazed that I couldn't subtract, divide, or multiply. While Ms. Jones stood in front the chalkboard in her living room trying to explain a math problem over and over that I didn't understand, her granddaughter Talia, who attended a nearby school, came home and made me look like shit, according to Mark. Everything that happened while at Ms. Jones's lesson, she reported to Mark or my mother, and since my mother arranged for Mark to pick me up on his way home, he got all the good and bad comments from Ms. Jones.

While we walked home, Mark used the bad comments to insult me and then changed the news to make it worse than it was when he told my mother so she could insult me as well. To Mark, I was a dunce and nothing was going to change his mind.

"How come you can't divide? Even Tailia can divide. You ain't a three-cent dunce, you're a dunce for real."

"Ms. Jones said I just have to work on them while I'm home. She said because it's my first day, so it's like a warm up day."

"You shouldn't be here in the first place. You should know all this basic math stuff. Anyway, you ain't my problem. Your mom will have to deal with you. Even Akhila could do that baby stuff, but you can't do it, why? Because nothing is up there. Your head is empty; there's no brain. Everyone has to help you do your work. It's like you're borrowing other people's brains because yours is not working. Trust me, it's a shame. You should be disappointed with yourself."

I couldn't say anything because he would have continued insulting me. People were looking, some were laughing as he embarrassed me and smiled along with the folks. I felt stupid. Mark told my mother that Ms. Jones said I didn't know anything at the lesson, and instead of finding out what happened to me, she took over where he left off. I thought, why is school so hard? Maybe Mark and Daddy are right, and I don't know anything. Everything I do is a failure. Every time my Mommy and Daddy get tired of me, they send me to these fucking people I hate.

My father and Mark persuaded me to believe that I was a dunce. I was only putting in the effort for my grandparents. They told I had to get into a good school so I could be somebody in society, even though I didn't understand the maths, or how to write a proper sentence; even science and social studies were somewhat of a problem. I didn't want them to continue to send me away because I wasn't behaving myself or doing what was required of me. I used to have homework, but pretended I didn't. Now, because I wanted to make my grandparents proud, when I reached my mother's house, I showed her I had homework and asked for help. The following day, I told Ms. Jones I hated mathematics and wished I didn't have to study with her, and she told my mother. My mother didn't beat me like my father did. Instead, she insulted me. I believed Ms. Jones really wanted to see me do well.

She once asked me, "Do you love to spend money?"

"Yes."

"Think about it. The money your parents give you, if you don't know how to count it, how will you know how much change to collect when you purchase something," she explained.

Ms. Jones insisted, in addition to my homework, I figure out fifteen things I use in my everyday life that requires knowledge of math. Before leaving the lesson, I had already written down ten of them without Ms. Jones knowing. The worst thing I could have done that afternoon was to asked my mother to help me figure out five other things I use in my everyday life that required mathematics, which I did.

"When Mark come home, he will do it," said my mother.

I wish I hadn't told this woman anything, I thought.

Whenever I asked my mother to help me with my homework, she always directed me to Mark. Then, when Mark came home, he grabbed the paper and finished the other five quickly and threw the paper in my face.

"These are simple thing you can't figure out. I don't know why they're wasting time sending you to school.

All I see you doing is heating the school bench, nothing else," said Mark, while Mommy sat in the opposite chair, laughing at me and watching Fresh Prince of Bel-Air.

I gathered my papers after picking them up from the floor, put them in my book bag, then spread the blankets they gave me on the floor and went to sleep. Mark and my mother woke me up the next morning discussing how doltish I was.

"Never in my life have I had to deal with someone so stupid," said Mark.

I cried for hours in their latrine while they were sleeping because of their insults.

On the weekend of my birthday, my mother and Mark thought it was wise for me to stay home and work on some school work, but my grandmother disagreed. She couldn't think of anything better than to send me home for the weekend. Bright and early Saturday morning, I left Port Rime, and that was the last time I saw Ms. Jones.

The second I reached home, I informed my grandmother about the way Mark treated me. She said I wasn't going back and that was final.

My grandmother was impressed with the amount of stuff I learned while attending Ms. Jones's lesson—addition, subtraction, multiplication, and breaking up words in syllables to figure them out and read sentences. The only thing I did not understand was division, but that was the last thing I wanted my grandma to find out. A few days after my birthday, my mother decided to take me out after having an argument with my grandmother. Mark suggested the Chinese restaurant was a great place to celebrate my birthday. When I arrived in Georgetown at New Driving Chinese Restaurant my mother, Mark, Akhila, his older brother, niece, and nephew were waiting for me. Before I could tell them what I wanted, Mark said since it's his money he's calling the shots. Mark bought one box of food fried rice, I didn't know if the food had meat inside, because I was at the end of the table and by the time the food reach to me, literally there was only three spoons of fried rice and plenty hot sauce.

The one liter of soda that Mark bought was passed one after another someone took a mouthful and past it to another person. Since I was the person I automatically thought the remaining soda was mine. I lean the bottle to my head and took a mouthful, Just as I was about to take a second mouthful Mark slap the bottle out of my hand. Some of the drink that left in the bottle went into my noise, spill on my face, clothes, the table and the floor.

"What the ass is wrong with you, how you gonna drink all the drink?" asked Mark.

"This boy does fret me, always lickrish," said my mother.

"I thought the rest was for me," I said softly, then cried.

All of a sudden, they begin shouting. Calmly, I waited until they were finished and then asked to go home. This was the only time in my life that my grandfather ever did the opposite of what I asked. After I informed my grandfather what had happened, I begged him not to say anything to my grandmother, knowing the confusion that would erupt. My grandfather said he wasn't going to say anything. But a few hours later, my grandmother and Aunt Kimberly were questioning me about the way Mark and mother had treated me. I could have been on the public road and heard my grandmother arguing with my mother, demanding to speak with Mark.

"If only Daddy didn't say anything," I said, but it didn't change my love for him.

It was a Friday afternoon, when Robert called saying my grandfather was rushed to the hospital. I cried, but not as much as my grandmother. Just before we walked out the door, the phone rang. It was another phone call concerning my grandfather, and my grandmother said Robert told her my grandfather was on his way home. She tried to call back Robert as a result of finding out what really happened, but Robert didn't answer until thirty or so minutes later. Robert said he noticed my grandfather's hand shaking while they were closing the door of the store. Soon after, while my grandfather was getting his stuff together to leave, he fell and hit his head, which was when Robert called the ambulance.

"I'm going by the road to wait on him," I said to everyone.

"Okay, go," my grandmother replied.

I cried while running to the public road, wondering, hoping, and praying to God for my grandfather to stay alive and feel better. After waiting twenty minutes, my grandfather arrived in a taxi. Before the driver could reach his hand beside his seat to open my grandfather's door, I helped my grandfather out. Although his foot was wrapped in gauze, he still wanted to walk on his own.

"Can you walk, Daddy?" I asked.

"Yeah, I'm okay," he replied.

"Are you sure, Daddy?"

"Yeah, son."

While walking, I kept close to him just in case he lost his balance, even though he wasn't comfortable.

"What you doing?" he asked.

"I'm making sure you don't fall."

"Do I look like an invalid? I don't need anyone help me walk."

I laughed and gave him his space, but I still kept an eye on him just in case something happened. When we reached the house, my grandmother started questioning Daddy concerning his condition. He was angry that the doctor told him he couldn't attend work until the wound on his foot healed. I was excited my grandfather was staying home until my grandmother lost her job too.

Next door, there's a rich family named the Millers. Mr. Miller is another man our community looked up to. My grandfather said that in his younger days our two families were close. Uncle Scott and Uncle Carlos were friends with Mr. Miller's two sons, Eli and Marcus, when they were small. After the two boys left Supply to stay with their mother in Georgetown, they all failed to keep the connection going. Without the Millers, we would have been even worse off after my grandparents lost their jobs. Whatever little we had vanished, but the Millers did what they could to help.

Mr. Miller helped us out with half of the payment for the light bill, and then it was our job to find the other half to ensure the lights stayed on. Sometimes, we had to let the light get cut off to buy groceries. Sometimes, Aunt Kimberly helped us out with the light bill and with groceries. No matter what, we couldn't afford to pay for water, so we had to fetch from our neighbor's out on the public road.

Every morning at four, my grandfather and I got up to fetch water for our everyday use. I never wanted my grandfather to come due to his condition, but trying to persuade him not to when he made up his mind wasn't easily done. So I would let him sit by the standpipe and

OUT OF THE JUNGLE

fill the bucket while I carried the full buckets to fill the bigger drums and then returned with the empty containers. By the time we were finished fetching water, it was time for me to get ready for school. As soon as school was over, it was my responsibility to hurry home so I can do any errands Ms. Miller wanted me to do. One day after helping Ms. Miller, I heard and then saw my grandmother shouting from our veranda.

"Ounga! Come quick! Come quick!" my grandmother shouted to the top of her lungs.

I ran as though I was being chased by a lion or some wild animal.

"Hurry up! Quick, boy!" said my Aunt Kimberly.

"Mommy is on the phone with your stepmother, what's her name?" asked Aunt Kimberly.

"Aunty Kate," I answered.

"Did you know Simon is going to the United States with Kate?" asked my grandmother, as she covered the mouth of my aunt's phone.

"No, but the last time I went by, Emma and Erica was talking about America and traveling on a plane."

"Right, right! She didn't directly say when they're leaving, but from the way she was talking, it sounded soon. But that's not all. She wants to put in for you and your brothers and sister," said my grandmother.

"So, we will all be going with them?" I asked.

"I don't know if y'all leaving the same time with them, but when she calls back, we'll know what's really happening."

We didn't receive another phone call until two something the next morning, informing us to be at Cheddi Jagan International Airport at four-thirty in the morning. When my mother, grandmother, and I arrived at the airport, we found out only Kate, Emma, Erica, Kasey, and Al were leaving the country at the moment. My father told my grandmother, he couldn't leave with Kate and the children because of Lina, I, and Riya, a younger sister I didn't know I had.

My father also needed to fix some documents we needed to travel. During the check-in for their flight, while Daddy helped Kate take in their suitcases, my mother caressed Emma and told her how much she would miss her.

"Don't worry, Ounga, is here with you," said Emma.

My mother kissed her and laughed as she hugged Emma. I went and stood next to my grandmother. Then, it was time for them to board their flight, and it was the first time I saw a plane close up. I waved as Kate, Erica, Emma, Kasey, and Al walked further into the airport.

"Okay! Now, that they're gone, I can work on these guys' passports," said my father.

"Where is the other girl?" asked my mother.

"She and her mother are on their way to meet me in Georgetown."

"Do you need me to come and help you with Lina and Junior?" asked my mother.

"If you want to, you can come."

"So it's just the passport you're getting them today?" asked my mother.

"Yeah, everything else can be prepare from the States," he replied.

When we arrived at the passport office, Riya and her mom, Melanie, were waiting on us. That was my first time meeting Riya and Melanie, but Lina said that when they were younger Riya visited them during the holidays. As we sat and waited to be called on, Lina and Riya were quizzing each other on various spelling words. I prayed that they didn't ask me any of the words, because I didn't have a clue how to spell Mississippi or photosynthesis; they sounded clever and more people around them began to tune in and smile. It was uncomfortable being there with my mother and father. I felt better being around my grandparents, but my grandmother was looking at the bigger picture.

CHAPTER 19

M y grandmother has a magnificent friend named Isabella. If I was to have a friendship with someone, it would definitely be a similar relationship with Isabella and my grandmother. They met at church; and in the midst of Bishop John's prayer meeting is where I first laid eyes on Isabella's daughter, Madison.

"She is so beautiful, so pretty," I repeated to myself all day.

I kept my eyes open during prayers, not thinking how angry it probably made God, so I could gaze at her charming face. From that day, I made it my duty to be in church every Sunday, and sometimes during the week if my grandmother went. As a result of being a dancer, Madison and the other church dancers sat on the opposite side from which I sat. But it never stopped me from admiring her, even sometimes when she fell asleep because Bishop John could bore some of us with his story.

I cried and begged my grandmother to attend the church's school that Madison and her two cousins attended, but unfortunately, her answer was no. It surprised me, but my grandmother spoke as gently as she could.

"Ounga, it's only because you're interested in taking part in the school that the church organized. Normally, you would've already got a belt lash to your head for asking a question like that, knowing the crisis we're going through," said my grandfather.

The following Sunday after church, everyone in our home found out why I was crying to attend Bishop John's Academy. I wrote Madison a love letter and left it on the table. As soon as I wrote the letter, I was supposed to put it in my bag, but my grandfather asked a favor of me, and I unconsciously set the letter down. By the time I returned, my grandmother had the letter in her hand and was waiting at the table.

"The boy is in love," shouted Uncle Carlos.

"Which Madison you in love with?" asked my grandmother, while I stared her as though she was crazy. "I hope it's not the Madison I know."

"Which Madison you know, Mommy?" asked Aunt Kimberly.

"Isabella's daughter. I just want you to know that Isabella's husband has a gun, and if he sees anyone around his daughter, he'll kill them; so, you could make a fool of yourself," said my grandmother, while everyone stood there and laughed at me.

"I doubt Madison would love a boy who doesn't like to brush his teeth and doesn't like bathe," said Uncle Carlos.

"If you like Madison, you would have to change a lot of things, boy."

"The girl doesn't want ugly, Ounga."

From the day they said all of those things, it was my duty to brush my teeth four times a day and bathe every time I felt hot in order to make sure Madison loved me in return. While my grandparents weren't working, Isabella gave us whatever little pastries she could afford to from her catering business. I couldn't've cared less about the pastries and clothes because Madison has been always there, and my intention was to see her. All she had to say was, "Hi," and everyone was curious about why I did everything I was supposed to, and more, without being told.

Unlike many other words describing anyone I admired, I chose to tell my best friend, Isaiah, "My girlfriend's name is Madison, and she is very pretty."

Isaiah and I became best of friends on my first day attending Supply Community High School. Many said it was a cowboy school because every student fought and cursed as they pleased. When my mother received my test scores from the Common Entrance Exam, she said the score wasn't low or high, but there was huge problem. My test scores didn't match the requirements of the schools Mark choose for me to attend, so instead of the Ministry of Education assigning me a school, we had to go out and search for one that I could get into. The people at the Ministry of Education said my parents should have chosen a selection of schools with varying requirements instead of only very good schools. But Mark was wicked and did it on purpose; he chose only the top schools in the country.

Supply Community wasn't on my wish list or the school I dreamed of attending, but Addy was going there, so I didn't mind. Also, Aunt Kimberly said it was going to save us money on transportation because it was so close to home. Ten percent of the time, Addy and I would walk to school; the other ninety percent, he stayed home. But when it was time to take an exam, he would show up and ace all his exams, getting better scores than students with perfect attendance, including myself. As a result of not being home as much as Addy, I begin to lose out on working for Ms. Miller. By the time I reached home, Addy had already run all the errands for her. Sometimes I got angry and went into her backyard where the fruit trees were and ate her fruit until I was satisfied. Whenever Addy stole her money and didn't want run her errands, that's when I was able to make a few dollars to buy bread and a can of condensed milk to survive.

After working for Ms. Miller one afternoon, Aunt Kimberly asked me to stay with Addy and Mia, one of my first cousins, until she returned. Without thinking twice, I agreed to keep them company in Peter's home. As soon as my aunt left, the plan was to go and swim in the river, but Carly stopped by. She ended up staying with us because she wanted to speak with Aunt Kimberly. Addy was always cool with Carly. He even told me he loved staying with her alone. Why? I never knew. While they were in the house playing music, I was in the garage admiring the Jet Skis, boat, and the four-wheeler.

"Yo, Ounga! Come quick," shouted Addy.

"Coming, Dee," I replied.

Carly and Addy were in the living room. Mia wasn't in sight.

"Yeah?"

"Carly wants to talk to you."

She smiled at me. "I just want to see if Mia's a good girl. She looks kinda slutty."

"No, she's not slutty," I replied.

"Which one of us will ask her?" Addy asked Carly.

"Come on, Addy. You'll have to do it. Ounga's her cousin, so she might say no. When she starts sucking your dick, Ounga will come in and both of you will sandwich her," said Carly.

At first, Mia didn't want to suck his cock, but after Carly took her into the room she returned ready. Mia unbuckled Addy's belt, unbuttoned his pants, took out his penis, and went down on her knees before sucking on his cock.

"You have to push back the skin to get a good grip," said Carly.

After a while, she was comfortably sucking Addy's penis.

"You have to suck Ounga's penis too," said Carly, but she refused.

Eventually, Carly instructed her to whine on him. Addy put her over the chair, took off her underwear, and I walked outside.

As I sat on the trailer, I heard Mia saying, "Stop! You're too rough."

"Girl, what's wrong with you? Move your hand so the boy can do his thing," said Carly.

"Tell him he has to go slow."

"Addy, you can't go so hard on the girl."

It wasn't long before Mia ran outside with her pants and panties in her hands, smiling. Addy said they were going for a swim.

"I know you're surprised, but I could see it. She's not a normal girl. You see what I was telling you, right?" asked Carly.

Without saying a word, I walked away.

Even since then, we have taken it further than it should have gone. When Addy sister, Andorra came to stay, she like me and he kept Mia. I was a couple of years older than Andorra, and she said I was nice to her. She reminded me of Madison.

I needed shoes to attend school because one of the shoes my mother bought me was missing its sole after a few wears. Thankfully, Isaiah gave me one of his pair. Isaiah's foot is a couple sizes smaller than mine, but still I accepted the shoes with a smile. It was better to walk with tight shoes than to wear one shoe and have your other foot touch the floor. I was, and still am, thankful for all the times Isaiah would buy me lunch when I was very hungry and never showed it. We had a couple of lean months where all I was promised was a slice of bread and a cup of tea before I went off to school. Some afternoons, I was lucky if Addy didn't want to work for Ms. Miller. She knew what we were going through, so after I finished the errands, she gave us her old bread that was supposed to been thrown out. Ms. Miller also told me to warm up the food she gave me to carry to my grandmother. Every time she gave us food it was always spoiled, but my grandmother continued to accept it.

"Mommy, how come Ms. Miller has so much good stuff and she gives us stale bread and food that is not good?"

"I know it's not nice or the best, but you have to remember they're helping us with our light bill. So, even though they might be bad in one way, they're good in another way. We have to overlook the bad."

"Is Mr. Miller helps us pay the light bill, not Ms. Miller."

"And who's Mr. Miller to Ms. Miller?"

"He is her husband."

"All right, then. So, that says they're one. Their household."

"We are bad lucky."

"You think we're bad lucky? There's some people going through way worse than what we're facing. Never tell yourself you're worse than anyone. There's always someone in a deeper struggle. What you have to do is be better, go to school and take in your education so your children won't have to face the struggles that you face. Okay?"

"Yes, Mommy."

"You're getting the opportunity to go and live in America. I think you should grab hold of that opportunity. There's a lot of people who wish they were going to America, but haven't got the opportunity. When you go there, you must do your very best. Whatever your aiming to achieve, do your very best to accomplish whatever that is. If you fall off track, get up back and keep going. Don't let nothing stop you, my son. Remember, only you can hinder your blessings. No one else can."

"I used to want to be a person who pumps, gas at a gas station because of the amount of money I saw the people in my country get from the customer. I told myself if I made so much money, maybe I can pay the light bill, water bill, and buy a big television. When I heard my stepmother was going to the United States of America, my plan was to become a singer."

"You never know! You become someone good, and Madison might end up liking you. Isabella wants someone who can look out and care for her daughter," said my grandmother.

I told Isaiah I was immigrating to America, and then I told Noah after a few weeks of being friends. The class thought Noah was a coward until someone older tried to fight me. It was soon after that I found out Noah lived just a couple of properties away from my grandparents.

We were best known in Supply Community School as the humble guys, Noah, Isaiah, and Rayfield.

Ms. Valentina, a wonderful teacher at Supply Community School, said she was curious to see the man I would grow into. I always told her someday you will see.

Everyday after school, Noah and I would wait on the school's bridge with Isaiah until he got transportation to travel home, and then we would walk home. Some days after working for Ms. Miller, I would go to Noah's house to hang out and eat whatever he cooked.

When my grandmother shared the news with Ms. Miller that I was immigrating to the United States, my grandmother told me Ms. Miller replied, "He will be coming back soon."

"I don't understand," I said.

"What do you think she mean?"

"When I go to America, I will come back?" I replied.

"She is trying to say when you go to the States, you will get deported."

"That is what Ms. Miller might wish for me, but it will not happen. I will be somebody."

"That's my son."

My father's oldest child, my Aunt Joy, received our visas from the American Embassy, and told my grandmother the embassy gave us six months to leave Guyana or else my stepmother would have had to refile for us to come to the United States.

"All Simon has to do is buy their tickets. Kate already did all of the hard work," said Joy.

"Can he afford to buy travel tickets for all of them?" asked my grandmother.

"He better."

"Ounga, excuse your grandmother and myself for a minute."

"Yes, Aunty Joy," I replied while they spoke as silently as a fly.

Other than my father's mom, Aunty Joy is another member of their side of the family who I really love. A couple of months before Riya, Lina, and I left, I was assigned four projects from Ms. Valentina. Each project was for a different subject, it was a mathematics, English, science, and social studies assignment. Ms. Valentina said instead of giving the class a final exam, she was giving us projects, which were fifty points each. After being added up, if an individual gets fifty on all of the assignments they will automatically get one hundred as a final grade. I have been happy with her decision because ever since the first test, I had never gotten less than seventy-five percent on anything, so those assignments were my final shot to raise my grades. Aunt Joy told me if my grades were really good, I will be put into a great high school, and with that I could attend a good college.

Before those four assignments, I had a few assignments

Aunt Joy and her daughter, Harmony, had helped me with. I scored a perfect grade on all of them. My plan was to ask Aunt Joy to help me again, but Harmony had a lot of schoolwork. After explaining the situation to Harmony, she suggested that I go to Guyhoc Park, where Aunt Patty could help me get the assignments done. Harmony said if Patty didn't have time and couldn't help me, then she will sacrifice her time to help me accomplish them.

I was only supposed to spend four days, but when Patty noticed how good I was when it came to cleaning and cooking, she extended my time there for two weeks. Every day I got up and cleaned the yard while her son was still sleeping. Then I helped her tidy the house and hung around until she asked me to take on another task. Before I left Supply, I forgot to take my toothbrush and, or towel because I assumed she had some for her guests. The only things I carried with me was my haversack, a couple shirts and pants, and my assignment's instructions.

I wanted a toothbrush to clean my teeth, but Patty told me to take the collar of my shirt, put some toothpaste on it and wipe my teeth. After bathing, I was told to dry my skin with the dirty clothes I took off. When my brief smell really bad and I had to change them, I asked her to buy me a couple, but she refused. Before Alton and Aston came home, Patty made sure I did all the work in their yard, which give the boys time to relax before they went and play with friends.

"If you want to be part of us, you must always listen and do as you are told,"

"Yes, Aunty Patty."

During the night, while Patty and her husband Roger slept on their bed underneath a mosquito net and the boys under theirs, I was used to distract the mosquitoes from attacking them. Patty said if Cousin Jerome wasn't up-stairs, I could have slept on Margarita's bed. They said he had tested positive with tuberculosis, and I couldn't be anywhere close to him because I had to travel soon.

After two weeks at Aunt Patty's, she decided she didn't understand most of the work. I was then sent to Aunty Joy's to complete my assignments. Harmony, who was also considered one of the smart ones, collected the instructions and understood everything that needed to get done. It took us seven days to complete all four as-signments, and on the eighth day, Aunty Joy drove me to school where we turned in the assignments. On our way back, she dropped me home and spoke with my grand-mother about things they didn't want me to know. It was the ladies' talk.

June 8, 2010, at eight in the morning was our check-in time at Cheddi Jagan International Airport. It was very exciting, but my heart was facing one of the most devas-tating times of my life. My grandfather told my grand-mother the night before that him going to the airport to see me, the best thing that ever happened to him, leave was too much for his heart.

Don't go, Ounga. Adam needs you, said the voice in my head.

I cried, but the decision to immigrate to the United States was made. Right after so much fun—like flying on a plane for the first time and feeling how cold New York was—it was six in the morning on Saturday, October 10, 2010, and I was returning home from the store when, for no reason, my grandfather came to mind. When I get a job, I have to buy Daddy couple boxes of insulin, oatmeal, powdered milk, and other stuff that's usable for someone who's diabetic.

About fifteen minutes later, when I walked into my father's apartment from buying bread and eggs, I had a phone call from Aunt Patty waiting. There was no "good morning," no "how are you doing," she just got straight to the point.

"Your grandfather died this morning. Your grandmother wants you to call as soon as you can. Sorry for your loss. Give your father the phone; I want to tell him something."

I felt numb. My legs shook uncontrollably. I fell to my knees in the kitchen beside the radiator and my heartbeat slowed. I wanted to cry, but there weren't any tears to weep. Instead, I felt a pain in my heart.

"God, please! This isn't true. Daddy is still alive. I didn't get to say goodbye."

I raised myself off the ground and went in the bathroom, locked the door, and took a seat on the toilet bowl. "I forgot to call him last week. What the fuck is going on? This is not true. This is not true."

Then, I went and asked my father for two dollars to buy a Hot Dog phone card. It was the first time he gave me money to call my grandparents when I asked him. When I called home, my grandmother answered the phone crying, and then I started to cry too.

"Hello?"

"It's me, Mommy, Ounga."

"Ounga?"

"Yeah, Mommy."

"I'm so sorry, but your grandfather passed away couple hours ago."

"Please don't say it," I cried.

"Granny is so sorry, baby."

"It's okay, Mommy."

"Is your father around?"

"Yeah, he's on the phone with Aunt Patty."

"Will your father send you home for the funeral?"

"I don't know, but I can ask him, if you want."

While my grandmother was speaking to me, I heard my uncles, cousins, even Aunt Kimberly shouts, "I want to talk to Ounga!" But my grandmother kept telling them to hold on.

"Don't ask him now. I don't want him to know I asked you to ask him. When the two of you are alone, then you ask him, okay, son?"

"Okay, Mommy."

"Tell everyone I said greetings."

"Okay, Mommy."

"Before you go, tell Kate I said thanks for everything,"

"Okay, Mommy."

"Is she home?"

"No."

"She gone to work already?" asked my grandmother.

"I'm not sure."

"How you don't know?"

"Aunt Kate don't live with us."

It wasn't what Lina, Riya, and I expected, but when we arrived at my father's apartment from John F. Kennedy International Airport, Emma was the only person in the house greeting us with a welcome home sign at the door. There was no sign of Aunt Kate, Erica, Kasey, or Al.

After unpacking my suitcase, I curiously asked my father, "Where is that little guy who couldn't wait to see me."

"He's with his mother. Don't worry, tomorrow after work we'll visit," said my father.

Later the following night, my father made arrangements with Emma for us to meet him at Church Avenue train station. When he arrived, we were on our way to see Al.

"We have a surprise for you guys," said Emma.

"What it is?" asked Lina.

"You'll find out at the right time," said my father.

"Come on! Tell me, please," begged Lina.

"Child, relax. When we get there, you will find out what it is."

"Thank you, Daddy. I think that's why it's called a surprise," said Emma.

About twenty minutes later, my father called to tell someone how close we were. I thought it was Aunt Kate or Erica, but when he handed me the phone, the individual's voice was unlike any voice I was familiar with.

"Hello Goodnight," I said.

"Hey Junior, how are you?" asked the person.

"I'm fine, thank you."

"Okay, cool, put Riya on the phone."

They lived on the second floor of a building similar to my father's. As my father knocked on the door, a little boy on the other side was shouting, "Daddy! Daddy! Daddy!"

I couldn't wait to see Al again. The little boy opened the door and ran outside to jump into Emma's arms, and a woman came out of the apartment with two other boys. When she spoke, I realized she was the woman I spoke to on the phone. I was looking for Al, Kate, Kasey, and Erica, but they were nowhere to be seen. While the girl and two boys stood beside my father, Emma, held the little boy and stared at him while he blushed, smiled, and hid his face every now and then.

"You're not going to say hi to Junior or Lina or Riya?" the little boy's mother asked.

"I don't know them," replied the little boy.

"You don't know this boy? Or these two girls, do you? Come on, Dante. You don't know? I told you about them," said my father.

Dante lifted his shoulder as if to say, "I don't know?"

"This is your big brother, Junior, and Lina, Riya, and Emma are your sisters," said my father.

He lifted his head up while smiling and whispered, "Hello," while waving his hand.

Everyone began to laugh, including myself, then Sabrina, Dante's mother, took us inside the apartment. She introduced us to her parents' in their room. After hugging Sabrina's parents, Emma, Lina, and Riya went into the living room where Sabrina's two brothers, Ryan and Will, were playing Call of Duty. As they hung out in the living room, I sat beside Mr. and Mrs. Clark's bed while they informed me they had lived in a town on the East Bank, Linden, before immigrating to the United States. Mr. Clark's wasn't interested in Guyana or the issues the country was facing, instead he was obsessed with how the girls were doing. Sabrina told my father, who mentioned Mr. Clark was soon traveling to Guyana. After I left their room, and I returned to the living room.

Every now and then Riya and Lina looked at each other, then at Emma and me, and then smiled. At first, I paid it no mind because whenever Riya and Lina were together they loved to fool around, but over time they begin to look weird. I knew they had something up their sleeves. I couldn't figure out what they were doing, but I thought whatever it was, Emma had a clue. Every time Lina and Riya looked at Emma and smiled, she would give one in return. Later that night, we returned home and as soon as my father fell asleep, Riya began questioning Emma for information concerning Ryan.

"I knew it!" Emma said with a smile.

"What?" replied Riya, blushing.

"I knew you liked Ryan!" yelled Emma.

"Girl, quiet! You want Daddy to wake up?" whispered Riya.

"And whose problem would that be? Not mine, I know for sure," replied Emma.

"Oh shit! It's about to go down. Riya is in love with Ryan," said Lina.

Riya leaned back in the chair, and looked up to the ceiling while smiling as though her feelings for Ryan had taken her breath away.

"You don't find it weird that you're in love with your stepmom's brother?" asked Lina.

"Who? Sabrina!"

"Yeah."

"She's not my stepmother. Aunt Kate is my stepmother," said Riya.

"Isn't Sabrina the woman sleeping with your father?" asked Lina.

"Yeah."

"Then, my child, Sabrina is your stepmother."

"You have to remember Aunt Kate is still married to Daddy, and Sabrina isn't, so Sabrina doesn't really count," replied Riya.

"Oh, really? You have a lot to learn."

"Preach, preach, my child, preach Lina preach," said Emma.

"I don't know what's wrong with her," said Lina while staring at Emma.

"Y'all making it seem as though Ryan is my blood family."

"No, my child! That's not the point I'm trying to make. What I'm really saying is that he's part of your family, so basically he's not someone you should want to be with," said Lina.

"Okay, Mommy," replied Riya sarcastically.

At first, I couldn't connect the dots, but if at any given moment Emma had the opportunity, whether it was my father told her or Sabrina asked her to go over to the Clark's, she went without making a commotion. When Emma was asked to do any other errand besides going to the Clarks, she always asked one of us to do it instead. I wondered why Emma wasn't calling or dealing with Aunt Kate. My father didn't like it when I spoke to Kate without his supervision. He was afraid Kate would tell me what happened to their marriage and why she wasn't living with us. In the morning, after my father left for work but before Emma woke, I secretly used her phone to call Kate. The first time we spoke, I thanked her for the opportunity she gave me.

Coming to the United States is the dream of many Guyanese; to step foot into the United States of America is their greatest joy. I have seen a bus driver who was a very close friend to my grandfather marry a woman he didn't know or love at the time just to set foot in the United States. Uncle Carlos told me how lucky I was to go to New York. He told me to send him a wife so he could get in on the opportunity, but that was before he found the woman of his dreams. I have seen the wall created between those who have gotten the opportunity and those who are less fortunate. Kate had not realized my father was just using her to get to the United States. The second time we spoke, Kate told me how Daddy broke her heart. Kate told me to never be a bad husband, to never be like my father. I promised her I wouldn't be.

Although Kate was living in the shelter with Erica, Kasey, and Al, she still came to hang out some afternoons, or to buy us clothes when the girls and I needed them. At first, my father was okay with the kindness Kate showed us, but after a few times, he said she was trying to show our relatives that he wasn't taking care of us. He made new rules that none of us could speak to Kate without him being present. The girls always obeyed him; I did the total opposite.

Once my father was on his way to work and the girls were still sleeping, I called Kate. At that time, she was always on the D train going to work. Some mornings I risked leaving the house to go to the station to see Kate when her train stopped at Church Avenue. Kate always had something to give me. There were a couple of times when I returned to the apartment that Emma was awake, and I told her I went to the deli to get a Halls lozenge, as a result of the cold I got after experiencing the cold of America. I told Kate everything that was going in his house. She was always curious about Sabrina and my father and how they treated us. Sabrina, on the other hand, did not want the girls and I to have any relationship with Kate. Every small and large incident that occurred, I informed Kate about. I told her not to tell him, and she said she wouldn't, but when they got into an argument, Kate insulted him about how much of a phony father he was.

The first time Kate and my father argued, he was at work. Half past noon, he called the house and told Emma to put the phone on speaker.

"Who was recently talking to Kate and told her about what is going on in my home?"

One after another we all said, "I didn't talk to Aunt Kate."

"You're sure?" he said.

"Yeah, Daddy" we said, one after another.

"Okay," he said, then he hung up his side of the line.

Later that afternoon, Daddy came home with records of all the calls we all made on Emma's phone. When my father walked into the apartment, in a very unhappy tone he called us to the front of the house.

"Who has been calling Kate early in the morning?"

The girls slowly said, "I don't know," while looking at each other.

"I was talking to Aunt Kate early in the morning," I said.

"Oh, it was you, but when I asked you earlier today, you said no."

I froze and didn't know what to say. Right then and there, he called me to closer to him, stood up out the chair, and slapped me.

"That's what you get when you lie to me. I don't want anyone talking unless they ask me when I'm home," said my father, as I held my face from the sting of the slap.

"I hope you haven't been telling her about my household, or else you will regret it."

My father said the only way Kate would know he wasn't buying groceries for us was if someone was informing her. Even if I hadn't told her, Kate had already known how much of a spiteful person he chose to be. Sometimes after being in a rage from arguing with Kate, Daddy only bought groceries when he needed food to eat.

At times when Daddy did buy groceries, he wanted the food to last us longer than it would have if we ate our fill. So, we stayed hungry and watch the food last until the rats ate it. When the rats got into some of the groceries, it made my father angry, but when that happened, he didn't curse, slap, kick, punch, or shout that he wasn't going to buy groceries for the month, that he'd rather have us starve.

I didn't take any of my father's warnings to heart; instead, I listened to my grandmother, who said, "Always keep in contact and do any little thing you can for Kate. Remember, if it wasn't for her, you wouldn't be in the United States."

I didn't mention what was happening to my grandmother, but I continued to call Aunt Kate at my own time and deleted the calls as soon as I was finished. I remembered one evening after work my father call while he was on his way home saying,

"We're going to have a long night, because my child is wearing a fucking mask, she wants to be a toy" then hang up the phone.

Lina began talking to herself saying, "Daddy doesn't have the right to beat her, because she didn't do anything wrong."

Riya was sitting in the living room shaking, I guess

the only thing that was bothering her was wondering if Daddy had found out that she had a crush on Ryan. There wasn't much to fear on my path, the fear was only new to them.

"Everyone stop what you're doing and get in the fucking living room," shouted my father as he entered the apartment.

Everyone drop what they were doing and reported to the living room like soldiers. No one asked questions, we just did what he said while he place his haversack on the floor beside the computer table.

"Do you know what this is?" asked my father while waving a sheet of paper in his hand.

"Junior, come on! Do you know what's this?"

"No, Daddy."

"Who was calling Kate?" asked my father.

"It was Junior," said Emma

"Is that true?" I stared at him as though he was crazy and didn't answer. "So you're the inside man?" he asked.

While I continued to stare at him as though he was talking to himself, my mind was already made up; if I was to get beat that night, I would stand there and let him beat me to death. Then I wouldn't have to see or worry about visiting him anymore. I can't die. I need to see Mommy and Daddy, I thought.

"You know, I always thought you would come and live with me, and we would do all the things we never did like father and son. You know, Junior, this might sound sad, but I should have let your mother abort you when I had the chance," said my father.

Even though that night we were all in trouble, I felt as though Daddy was angry and hated me for problems he should have.

"Y'all have a seat, make yourself comfortable. This paper is a record of the text messages and phone calls made from Emma's phone. A lot of the phone calls made were deleted, but thanks to the company, everything was recovered. Junior, Lina, and Riya I don't like it when my children lie to me. It drives me crazy, and there can and will be serious consequences. I'm going to make Emma an example." He turned to the girls. "Lina and Riya, y'all have boyfriends?"

They both look at each other and answered, "No."

"Lina, how many boys can you have at once?" he asked.

"One."

"Okay, that's believable. Y'all sister on the other hand is a sweet girl. The hottest woman in Franklin D. Roosevelt High School; that's what you are right?" asked my father.

"No," Emma sadly replied.

"No, don't say no; that's just what it is. In one of the messages, she told a boy that she wanted to be with him. So the boy asked her about Michael, the boy she claims to love. This little whore, I have for a daughter told the boy, 'What Michael don't know can't hurt him.'"

Though surprised by what the message said, I was shocked Daddy called Emma a whore.

Daddy's expression said it all, and the more annoyed Emma was, the angrier he became until he lost it. Daddy folded the stack of papers in his hand and lashed Emma on her mouth, before sulking in the corner where his bed was. While helping Emma clean the blood on her lip, Daddy returned with his belt. As I gathered the dirty tissues to throw them out, Daddy stopped me and asked, "What you think you're doing?"

"Emma's mouth was bleeding, so I just helped her clean the blood," I replied.

"Who's you?" he asked.

"I don't know."

"Who the fuck is you?" he shouted.

"Ounga."

My father wanted to say something, but for some reason he paused and bit his bottom lip. As he looked into my eyes, I could see his rage and hatred releasing. The muscles in his jaw flexed and his eyes went red.

"You think this is the first time I'm talking to Emma about boys? Emma behaves like a fucking whore," said my father.

If only my grandmother had known Daddy is still the same, I thought.

For that weekend, I refused to communicate with my father. If he was ever there when I woke, all he heard was a good morning and sometimes an evening greeting. Emma on the other hand, my heart had given in to her.

"Why?" I continued to ask myself as many other situations concerning boys occurred.

"You're crazy," Kate said. "Remember when Simon used to beat you, and how Emma used to laugh at you? Now you're lying and getting beat for her. It's nice that you're representing your sister, but she will not learn what your father is trying to teach her. Erica used to lie for Emma and keep secrets, but when Emma was confronted by her father, she told her father the truth, making Erica look foolish."

It was my decision not to listen, so whatever consequences were there for me to endure, I had to endure it. In the midst of my quiet moments while meditating, I reflected on Kate words about Emma laughing at me when my father beat me as a young child. Emma persuaded me into believing there was a reason for her actions and that I shouldn't believe Kate. Emma said they were all liars. The next boy situation, I was in was with her and Sabrina's oldest brother, Will. Her plan was for me to persuade Daddy into believing she and Will weren't in a relationship. Emma told me he's going to ask me if I noticed or suspected anything between them.

"Your job is to say no to everything that requires a no," said Emma

"What do I have to say yes to?"

"Daddy don't ask questions that require yes," said Emma.

"What about the phone records?" I asked,

"He's not going to find anything. I don't use my cell phone to contact Will, only the pay phone and he can't check that, only the government."

"What if he asks the government to print him a record?" I asked her as we sat on the bed.

"Junior, he doesn't have the time or the money to do that."

"So, you like Will?"

"Correction, my child, it's more like love."

"Okay, how old is he?"

"Only a year younger than I am"

"So, he is seventeen, right? And he's the only boy you're seeing, right?"

"Yeah."

My grandmother told me, "Everything happens for a reason. God doesn't make mistakes."

I saw what Kate was trying to tell me, but I believed trying to represent Emma in the time of her problems would better our relationship as brother and sister. Only when Emma got in trouble was I noticed or did she want to deal with me. All other times, it was her and Daddy's girls. Sometimes when members of their Jehovah's Witnesses meeting invited the youths on a fun day event, Emma always told them I couldn't make it or I was in another state, just so I couldn't take part. Thoughts of turning my back on them and returning to my grandmother went through my mind every time she did it. Every time I called home after the death of my grandfather, life got harder and harder for my grandmother.

During the summer, Erica, Kasey, and Al came daily to see us from the shelter they stayed at since Daddy had put them out. Erica was the only one who felt sorry for me when Emma turned the girls against me. For months, Daddy would cut Al's and his own hair, and give the girls money to do their hair. But no matter how high and hard my hair got, he always told me to comb it, even when I told him my head hurt.

The little money Erica got from her mother, grand-mother, and uncle she lent me to cut my hair, buy briefs, a Du rag to train the little bit of waves I accumulated, and food when they left me hungry. When my grand-father died, I couldn't go to Guyana for the funeral be-cause Daddy said he didn't have any money. I cried daily, mostly at night. Emma and my father couldn't have cared less. Not even the death of my grandfather softened their hearts toward me.

When Erica came to visit, she tried to cheer me up. At first, the kindness she showed me didn't make me feel better, but along the way she mentioned, "You said your grandfather really cared for you like his own grandchild, even like his own child. You said he showed you love, that he loved you like a son and greater. You guys shared the best moments with each other. You said you didn't get to thank or repay him for all things he did for you, but I believe you can. Grow and be the man he would have wanted you to become."

From that day on, I didn't cry. I overlooked how sad, angry, and stupid Emma and my father made me feel and continued to do what I needed to do to better myself.

Since my father was the one working, as his children and the dependents, he said our job was to prepared his food and make sure he caught the train on time in the morning. While Emma made a hot cup of tea alongside a couple of Crix crackers with peanut butter. Lina ironed his work shirt, pants, and tie, and Riya kept track of the time. I had no choice but to take the last job, which was to swipe my father onto the train with my school metrocard. As soon as Emma finished packing his haversack, I put it on my back and waited at the apartment door for him. While he put on his shoes, he told me to make sure I was ready to run down the stairs, through the lobby door, around the block, into the train station and swipe my metrocard, then I'd hand him his haversack while he walked through the turnstile.

There were times he missed his train, which made him late for work, but it was a result of him not going to bed early enough to wake on time. Since I was the last person that dealt with him those mornings, when Daddy missed his train, I got blamed. Some mornings, Lina weren't finished ironing his clothes on time, or Emma took her precious time buttering the crackers, or Riya fell asleep instead of telling him the time so he could move faster. I did my part right, but still got blamed.

In the afternoon when my father came home, he released his anger by shouting, then slapping, kicking, or punching me. When he got paid or received a tax return, everyone except me enjoyed it.

One summer evening, after returning home from Kate's family reunion in New Jersey, Daddy surprised the girls with a new bunk bed. The bed was a gift for their hard work and for being loving and supportive children. I was promised a new bed too, but until then I had no choice but to sleep on the old bed, which was infested with bed bugs, or the cold floor. While Emma slept comfortably on the top bunk with Lina and Riya on the bottom, I was tormented and frequently woke up in pain from a bug bite. Some nights I tried to kill the bedbugs as they revealed themselves, but other times seeing the amount of blood they had consumed from me was too disgusting.

When the bites got overwhelming, I spread the sheet on the floor to have a peaceful rest. Although the floor was hard and cold, I was free from bites. Though I did appreciate having somewhere to sleep. A few times, the thought of putting some of the bugs in their bed had toured my mind, but I didn't; my grandfather would have been disappointed with me. Making them feel how I felt wouldn't have made my grandmother or grandfather proud or make me rest better at night. It probably would have made my father even angrier, which would have put groceries on strike longer than a month.

When family members visited my father's home and asked him how the children were doing, he said, "The kids are doing great, except for Junior. The boy is ungrateful and selfish."

After a long time, the way I was being treated became unbearable. When I was supposed to swipe my father onto the train, I pretended to be asleep with the bed bugs. His alternative was Riya. So, she stood at the door with her school metrocard waiting for him to say, "Riya, let's go."

Whenever Daddy missed his train while Riya was helping him, somehow it was still my fault. There was one morning when Daddy couldn't find his metro-card, and I got slapped, kicked, punched, and stomped with his ACG Nike work boot.

My father accused me of stealing it, but a couple of hours after the commotion was over, and I was crying in the bedroom because of the pain in my ribs, he found the metrocard in the shirt he had worn the previous day. One of the things I disagreed with my father about was that once he had finished beating me, he expected me to for-get all about it. A couple of days after the incident, Kate told him he was going to have to stop beating me because I was a big boy. Daddy told her that I'm his son and he could do whatever he wanted with me.

CHAPTER 20

J ust a few weeks after Sabrina's parents and her two brothers moved out of their apartment and into her grandmother's house in East New York, Daddy decided he wanted to give up his apartment and live with Sabrina in the apartment that had been given to her. He told us it would be better for us to live there with her. I couldn't care less, but Emma was curious why he said her apartment was better.

"The rent, light, and gas bills are cheaper, and their apartment is in better condition than this old crap where you have to beg the people in charge to fix something," he stated.

The only person among us who was happy and thought it would be great fun was Riya. She wanted to reunite with Ryan and Sabrina, while Emma became jealous.

"Before Riya came to America, I use to help the bitch out, whether it was babysitting Dante or keeping her company," said Emma.

Lina couldn't have cared less; she was neutral with everyone. She didn't want to live with Sabrina, but when Daddy said we had to go, Lina just had to follow. Time and time again, I thought, why did we leave our happy family in Guyana to be involved in the Daddy's reckless-ness in America?

My father believed I caused the problems for him and Sabrina. Sabrina told him I would call Kate and discuss how wicked she is for sleeping with Daddy since he was a married man. I never told her, but we did. What else was more depressing and interesting to talk about?

Daddy told the girls they needed to pack up their stuff to move, and that was the only time he didn't go hard on them for something that benefited him. Daddy told me we were moving separately from the girls because he want-ed the girls to check out the rooms that were available, choose whichever they loved, and then I was to be given what they didn't want. How did I know? The girls told me. So I didn't take his offer, or help my father take our household items to Sabrina's apartment. I knew if I didn't go with them I would stay in his apartment until rent was due, then I would have gone home with Kate.

I was happy to be alone in my father's apartment until I ran out of food. I had no choice but to call him, and he directed me to her apartment. He always said she had all the good food at her place. Daddy used to yell at me for how stupid Sabrina said he was in helping his kids get to America and in the end, we turned our back on him. According to Sabrina, I was a heartless ungrateful dog. Sabrina always created a problem with whoever she felt was against her. If at any time I went over to Sabrina's apartment for food and walked into the apartment without greeting her, even if I had forgotten, Sabrina started up an argument with Daddy that ended with him punishing me.

Sometimes when I went over for food, Sabrina hurried and gave me whatever was left over just to get rid of me. When I realized Lina and I were eligible to receive food from school, unlike the students whose parents could afford to pay, I made it my duty to make sure Lina and I were always at BCA for breakfast and lunch, that way I didn't have to beg my dad and Sabrina for much. The other students that attended BCA gossiped that I ate like a football player, that I ate enough for two grown folks. I never got mad because they didn't understand why I ate so much. Those students did not understand how it felt not to know what they were going to eat when they got home after a long day of school. Whenever I got a few bucks from Kate, I bought a two-dollar Hot Dog card to call my grandmother in Guyana.

Every time I called, my grandmother always said how much worse the cost of living was becoming in Guyana, and I felt heartbroken to tell her there was nothing I could do to help her out. Just to get her mind off the sadness of my grandfather's death, I would always mention to her how hard I was trying to get good grades so I could someday get a good job and bring her to the States to live happily ever after. Sometimes, I thought about my grandmother leaving me the way my grandfather did and cried for hours, but in the midst of the sad feelings, a voice in my head always gave me a vision of brighter days.

"Ounga, baby, make me proud."

"I'm going to make you the proudest grandmother in the world," I promised.

Whenever I felt discouraged, her inspiring words were all I needed to hear.

"It doesn't matter what people think about you, whether it's good or bad, at the end of the day what matters is what you think about yourself. Always remember where you came from. Don't hold on to it, but grab hold of the places you're striving to go."

I never forgot it, even when I didn't have money to call her, I wrote those words down on a paper and said it to myself as if my grandmother was saying it to me. Even when I felt hungry, I didn't mind eating food once I read my grandmother's inspirational note. I started researching the process it takes to become a pilot. Lina was curious why I choose a pilot. I explained it to her, though I knew she wouldn't understand.

"Throughout my whole life, I've been wishing for one thing or another, so being in the clouds would help my spirit stay awake."

When Lina told Daddy while they were discussing what they all wanted to become, she said my father said I was ungrateful and that I wouldn't become anyone great or make it in America without his help.

"Fuck him! Someday he's going to need me. I don't need his help. I can get what I need from school. I'll show him. He's more fucked up than I am. He had such a good family, all the people from Kate's family supported him, and helped him and his kids come to this country; and the second he came here, he turned his back and showed all of his fucked up and ungrateful ways," I said to Lina.

What he said made me so angry that I cried, but my grandmother's inspirational note got me back on track. I know I couldn't hold on to the bad and ugly way my father made me feel, so I programmed my mind to turn his comments around and prove the opposite. Still, I couldn't remove the hate I felt for him at the time, so I blanked him out when I was in school, and when I felt as though I was one step closer to my dream. Every now and then, I used to let the sound of my father's voice get into my head, especially when I started school at Brooklyn College Academy in the ninth grade. According to his voice, I was the one who didn't understand how to solve a division problem and was fit to be a dunce. At that time it all felt real to me, because the more he talked, the worse I felt about myself. The only reason I didn't believe I was a dunce was because I hated him, so I didn't care what my father said.

He used to teach the girls, including Sabrina, how to do the math problems they had trouble with or the ones they had for homework. There were times when my father invited me to join them, but I never felt comfortable. The girls understood what my father was teaching because they were able to concentrate. I was only thinking about the history we had. My father would call us out, one after the other, to work a made up problem based on what we were learning. When he called on me, that's when the apartment changed from a teaching atmosphere to cursing, slapping, punching, kicking, and belt-beating. Then, it all ended with him and his smart kids watching television.

Time after time of being beat down by my father for the mathematics problems, I stopped participating with them. I told my father Ms. Grons said I needed to work on my reading comprehension. Ms. Grons said she would help me with the math, and I accepted her help because she is much calmer. Ms. Grons taught at BCA Brooklyn College Academy and worked with children who had immigrated from other countries and were having a hard time understanding the US teaching system, students who needed extra help and their confidence to uplift. Well, that's what she did for me; Ms. Grons helped me build my confidence. She said you can be anything you want in the United States of America, but you must work to the best of your ability.

Every morning after breakfast and before I went to class I stopped by Ms. Grons room to go over some spelling words she gave me from the newspaper. Every afternoon when Ms. Grons finished helping Lina and I with our homework, she would have me read a paragraph from the newspaper or sometimes a history book. Ms. Grons said since she helped me finish my homework, when I got home, my job was to find the meaning of the words that I didn't know either from the newspaper or the history book. Ms. Grons said learning the meaning of the words would enhance my vocabulary. When I was in Ms. Gron's room with free time to spare, I told her how Guyana is different from New York City. As much as I wanted to tell her about the drama I was facing at home, I couldn't. The police would have arrested him for beating me, and if he wasn't locked up for good, he would have killed me when he returned home.

On September 2011, I took Ms. Cole's art class; the first and largest art class I had ever taken with approximately forty-five to fifty students enrolled. Although I tried to fit in by pretending to speak as though I was born and raised in New York City, every now and then I unconsciously used my Guyanese accent. For instance, when I was explaining a sketch I did of a model Ms. Cole brought into class, I talked about the number three, but accidentally said tree, and the whole class started laughing.

In reference to the cartoon, some students started calling me Ed, Edd, n Eddy because I had a head. Sometimes I laughed along with them to make it look like I wasn't hurt or humiliated. Just when I thought it couldn't get any worse, Ms. Cole asked for a volunteer to read a paragraph from the syllabus. I made eye contact with Ms. Cole, and she asked me to volunteer. I was super nervous and picking corn. After I finished there was a long pause, then Ms. Cole asked me what I understood from the paragraph.

Another student shouted, "Nothing."

In December, after giving everyone their report card, Ms. Cole looked me in the eyes and said, "You can and will do a lot of great things through your artistic abilities and talent."

I replied with a smile. Later that day while in the computer lab, I researched what artistic abilities meant. This woman is crazy! I thought. "Ain't nobody want to be an artist". Maybe that's what every teacher does persuades their students to follow in their choice of career.

After returning from Christmas break, every weekend the take home assignment Ms. Cole gave the class was to draw human body parts. Even though she gave the weekend to get the drawings done, I never started them until Sunday night and, as always, I received A's for each and every drawing.

"I can see you as the next Jean-Michel Basquiat," she said.

"Who is that?"

"A very famous and talented artist. He would have been a legend if he hadn't died."

"How did he die?"

"Heroin overdose."

"What's heroin?"

"A dangerous street drug. Do you know cocaine?"

"Yes."

"Well, it's like ten times worse."

"That's sad."

"It is."

"My grandmother told me to never say I want to be like anyone, and to always say I would love to be better."

"I don't understand."

"You said I will be like Jean-Michel, but I don't want to die the way he died."

"When I say I see you as the next Basquiat, I don't mean you will follow in his footsteps, but that I see a similarly talented artist in you."

"Okay. But are you serious I could be that talented?"

"Yeah, of course, with hard work and dedication. You just have to believe in yourself, and everything will fall into place."

"Okay."

"Keep practicing. That's the only way your artistic skills will improve."

Not only did I continue drawing, but I started writing poems. For every drawing I drew, I wrote a poem. I took every poem, drawing, and painting I completed and showed Ms. Cole. Some of the poems I wrote, Ms. Cole spoke highly of, and the others needed more practice and grammar correction. The poems that needed to be corrected I took them to Ms. Grons. Before Ms. Grons and I corrected the poems, she told me always keep room for criticism.

"The criticism might not sound pleasant," she said, "but it will help you see your mistakes, correct them, and grow."

On June 12, 2012, I was nominated for a Henley medal at the Metropolitan Museum of Art. Ms. Cole said out of six hundred students, only a girl from the twelfth grade and myself from the tenth were nominated. Everyone in BCA was so proud of me, and for once in my life, I felt like a hero, a Brooklyn College Academy hero. Then, on

June 14, I won the Henley medal. Not a single person from my household, including Lina, knew I had won. On the day of the show, I persuaded Lina not to attend school so she wouldn't know what I was up to. My father wasn't aware of the event because I couldn't tell him. My father didn't want to know I was doing anything that made me stand out, look talented, or seem smart. In my father's eyes and throughout his entire family, only he could be considered the best.

Around one o'clock, Ms. Cole and I left the school and were on our way to attend the ceremony. While traveling on the train, I told Ms. Cole that she was right; I was on my way. When we arrived at the Met, there were hundreds of students from all over New York. I never forgot that feeling of love, hope, and joy. I was proud to be nominated. I was very nervous, and told Ms. Cole I had never been awarded for anything. She told me live in the moment.

Indeed, that was a beautiful day. Ms. Cole introduced me to Katrina, the twelfth grade girl, and some of the instructor of the museum, who Ms. Cole said she knew from graduate school. I spoke to students from other schools and they loved my Guyanese accent. Although we were all there because we were nominated, everyone I met was proud of me and wished me good luck. I said the same to them.

When I arrived home, I hid the Henley medal in an old

shoebox where I kept my briefs. When Erica came over the following day, I showed her the medal. She smiled, told me keep the good work up. I was still struggling academically in school. I kept going to tutoring, and got extra help from Ms. Grons and Erica. Erica understood what I said when I told her there was a voice in the back of my head that stopped me from doing well on my tests.

"What voice?"

"I believe it's Daddy's voice because of how he used to tell me how much of a dunce I am. Well, any time I'm about to take a test, that's all I hear."

"You believe it?"

"I don't know. I try not to, but the voice takes over."

"You better stop listening to it. You're much greater than what the voice says. We were here in America before you, Lina, and Riya came, and not one of us have ever gotten an award. You just got here and already have one. Don't listen to your father's stupid's voice. Listen to your grandmother's voice. Make her proud."

"Okay."

"Congratulations, smart and talented Junior."

Erica came over often to help Lina and I with our homework. She helped me study for my tests too, and I began to improve. My test scores weren't the best, but they were better than before, and I thank her for that.

At the end of the school year for both ninth and tenth

grades, I received awards from my English, math, science classes as the most improved student. Ms. Kay, the assistant principal, sent a letter to my father's address so he knew about the award ceremony. I didn't expect him to show up, but he did after work. He didn't congratulate me; the only thing he said to me was that I should have gotten one for global history. My father then went on to say I should have made it onto the honor roll, because that's where he was in college. When we got home, he told the girls how proud he was of me and that I got those awards through hard work. I was irate. I didn't want him to talk about my work; he didn't know anything about my hard work.

In the eleventh grade, I took my first college class, which was psychology. My professor Ms. Saley, who was a psychologist, but loved to draw, paint, and sculpt, got along very well with Lina and me. The first time we spoke, Ms. Saley showed me a couple paintings she did and sold for a couple of hundred bucks.

When I showed Ms. Saley my work, she informed me that, "An artist never tells another artist how good their work is, but I'll make an exception for you; that's some pretty stuff you got there."

When I showed her the poems, Ms. Saley asked me if I love to write.

"Just poems. I'm not so good at writing essays."

"Do you have any short stories that you've written?"

"No, only poems."

"You're going to college right?"

"I think so."

"Why do you think so instead of being sure?"

"It's a long story."

"Is everything okay?"

"It's fine."

"You're sure?"

"Yeah."

"What's your name again?"

"Rayfield Douglas Walker"

"Douglas, like Frederick Douglass?"

"Yeah."

"Can I call you Ray?"

"Yeah, Ray is cool."

"Okay Ray, I won't say this if I didn't believe you should go to college because you're talented and smart. How long you have been writing poems?"

"I started that and the drawings at the beginning of last semester."

"If I had to guess how long you've been drawing, I

would have said you had probably started at a very young age to have become so good," she said. "What's your major?"

"You mean what I want to study when I go to college, right?"

"Yeah."

"Fine Arts."

"I think you should keep pushing yourself to become better. In college, it's important to have a major and a minor. That way, if one thing doesn't work out, you always have something else to fall back on. What else are you thinking about doing?"

"I've been thinking about films, so screenwriting, directing, and maybe acting."

"Mr. Walker, you took screenwriting right out my thoughts. The reason I think you should study screenwriting as a backup plan in college is because there's a lot of feeling within your work. Someone who's sad as a result of something can read this poem and feel better."

I didn't know what to say.

"I know it's a lot to take in, but I'm talking from experience."

I told Ms. Saley about Ms. Cole, and how she was the first person to see talent in me, and then she asked about my dreams.

"In Guyana, where I was born, my dream was to become someone who pumps gas at a gas station."

"What? That was your dream?" She looked aghast. "Why that was the only thing you were striving to become?"

"While I was in high school, my diabetic grandfather got sick for a couple months, and he couldn't work, so everyday life got harder and harder. I hardly went to school. Most of the time, I worked for our neighbors, or sometimes I assisted my aunt's husband with the daily work he did to help out my grandparents. One of our neighbors in Guyana always wanted me to buy gas for her. Every time I went to the gas station I saw the worker handling enough money to provide us with three square meals a day, and one of my best friends had the same job to help pay his mother's light bill."

"How old were you at that time?"

"Twelve, thirteen, around that age." I wanted to share more about my journey with her, but her face had already gotten red, including her blue eyes.

"Are you going to be busy this summer?" she asked.

"I'm not sure. I might have to go to summer school."

"If you're not going to summer school, you might want to check out this place out. It's called the Maysles Documentary Center. The team there specializes in teaching students how to make short films. I think you should check it out."

"I will, thank you."

"Good! Because I can see you're going far with this."

"I got you."

"Okay, Ray, I have to go now, so I will see you tomorrow."

Immediately after speaking with Ms. Saley, I ran to my guidance counselor, Mr. John, to find out what I could do to make the next year different from the previous one. He said I wouldn't have to go to summer school because I was doing well, but I had to retake the global regents for the third time. My hands went cold, my stomach began to hurt, and I felt sleepy.

"Don't worry, Mr. Walker. I'm sure this time around you will past the global regents. You would normally have to attend the summer class to study for the regents, but if you promise me you will study at home, I will excuse you from the summer class."

"I will, Mr. John. I promise."

"Okay, I believe you." He paused. "Why do you ask? Are you going to Guyana for the summer?"

"No, my psychology professor just told me about a film program she thought I would enjoy this summer."

"But I thought you were more into the fine arts?

That's media studies."

"I would also love to do screenwriting too."

"For movies?"

"Yeah."

"I know I've said it a thousand times, but with all the things you're pursuing, you remind me of a Renaissance artist."

"Thanks again," I said with a smile.

"I'll excuse you from the summer global practice, but you have to find another way to study for the regents."

"I will."

Ms. Grons and Ms. Beverly, the government teacher who loved literature, said I would help make the world better and have a positive impact on the lives of a lot people. The positive way people described my future kept getting better and better.

CHAPTER 21

"Junior, I don't know if I will live to witness it, boy, but you will go places and do things you never thought you could. All you have to do is stay on this path, and God will change your life; not only for yourself, but for others," said Kate's mom, who I now called Granny, while praying one day.

When I was in need of art supplies, Granny was the one who gave me whatever little money I needed to buy sketchbooks, drawing pencils, and watercolor paints after returning from work on the weekends at Kate's home. Whenever I did a drawing or painting while Granny was around, she asked questions about the colors and shading from the time I started to the time I finished. My father did the opposite. I was told by Kate to visit my father and show him some of the drawing and painting I had done.

"You never know, maybe this is your chance to connect and build a good relationship as a father and son," said Kate every time.

Even though whenever Kate sent me to build a relationship with my father, he turned me down and treated me like crap, I still had faith in Kate's words and in my father. I didn't understand after all the things that my father did, why she still tried to persuade me that he was a good man. Although I had lost all hope of building a father and son relationship, I took her advice and visited to show him the talent I had discovered within myself. As I walked on the sidewalk in front of their apartment building, my mind led me to believe my father and Sabrina had already seen me through their front window, and were maybe wondering what I wanted.

As I walked into through the lobby and up the stairs, it was as if the walls were whispering, why is Junior here? He betrayed his father and rather live with Kate. How sick!

Knock knock.

"Who is it?" asked Riya.

"It's Junior," I replied.

As I walked into their apartment, it was as if they had forgotten me entirely. On the wall were photos of everyone except me, and there was the quote, only those that love us never leave our side.

"What? You need something?" asked my father.

"No, I just wanted to show you some of the things I've been working on."

"Hurry, I have things to do."

I took out my portfolio with the drawings and poetry to show him. When I gave him the portfolio, he refused and said, "You flip the pages."

As I flipped through a few pages my father said, very annoyed, "How much more time you got? When are you leaving? Put it back in your bag. I will see you another day."

"Okay, Daddy."

I wasn't upset as I walked out the door; all I said was, "I told Kate."

When I arrived at Kate's house in the Bronx, I told her what my father did. Kate got angry, but I was confused. I wasn't the only person aware that a meeting with my father would have turned out that way. Uncle Nathan also said he knew it all along.

Everyone said that since Daddy broke Kate's heart and put her, Erica, Kasey, and Al out, he and Uncle Nathan were no longer best buddies, but terrible enemies.

"Simon is a fucking jackass," said Uncle Nathan any time someone mentioned Daddy.

The following week, Granny came to visit, heard what was going on, and decided to give my father a call. Granny cursed him out and then asked him why he treated me so badly.

Granny said my father told her, "You know I don't like boy children."

"Beside Junior, he has two other boys and he gets along fine with them. All the time, he takes out Al and Sabrina's son. He kisses them and tells them he loves them."

"I guess it's just Junior he has a problem with," said Uncle Nathan.

Uncle Nathan told Kate when he was going home to Brooklyn that he would love for me to go with him, just for a couple of days. I guess at first Kate was okay with the decision her brother made because I needed a father figure to guide me, but after a few weeks they kept calling to inform me of how ungrateful I was. I didn't know I would have been missed that much.

Uncle Nathan lived in Vanderveer Projects. Nathan lives with his son, Dexter, and from what I understood Uncle Nathan was supposed to be the father I never had, and Dexter fit himself in as my brother. One night, while Dexter and I were cooking, he mentioned how much he hated his father and wished Uncle Nathan was better. I thought for a second Dexter was losing his mind. The boy had everything he wanted and needed—a phone, video games, money, a bike. Uncle Nathan told Dexter how much he loved him, sometimes gave a kiss, and Dexter even had a birthday party every year. I told Dexter I never had a cake, much less a birthday party.

My grandparents could not afford to celebrate my birthday. I asked my mother to bake me a cake, but she never did. Only my other siblings got want they wanted for their birthday. My mother always brought Kentucky Fried Chicken for Emma and Lina on their birthdays at school. My mother made me watch them eat; Emma always preferred to share with her class friends. Lina had her birthday lunch while she was home, as her birthday was during the summer break. Even if I was to go home for some birthday lunch, by the time I got there, my two cousins would have finished the food.

Dexter didn't reply; he stayed silent for the rest of the night. As much as I needed a father figure in my life, sometimes Nathan's ways of dealing with life and becoming a man were too complicated, according to Dexter, but I didn't mind. Anything for an act of love, even if it turned out fake. From the time we woke up, he commanded us to make breakfast, then lunch. Since he was the person spending the money, he always said Dexter and I had to abide by his rules. Whenever he shouted at us, Dexter informed me how badly Uncle Nathan had beaten him numerous times.

"Don't worry, Junior. Daddy shouting at us is the little stuff. Whenever I get my father mad by doing anything he dislikes, he beats me like a criminal. Only Jesus himself could stop Daddy if he gets a hammer, belt, pat spoon, or anything that carries weight," said Dexter.

Dexter and I sat in the living room one afternoon talking about Uncle Nathan's bossy and clumsy attitude. We thought Uncle Nathan was at work, but instead he was outside in the hallway listening in on our conversation. As we laughed and talked, walking around discussing how stupid both Uncle Nathan and Daddy were, the door opened and he walked right in. Uncle Nathan had an angry look on his face; I was in shock because I thought Dexter was going to get beat, but Dexter said there was no way he could have heard, claiming the door was soundproof.

Whenever Uncle Nathan asked, once it was in my power to complete the task there wasn't anything on earth that could have stopped me from getting what he wanted done. Whatever it was, the tasks were completed just the way he wanted it. But according to Granny, he could be spiteful when things didn't go his way. Uncle Nathan often took Erica, Kate, Kasey, Al, Granny, Dexter, and Acacia to the movies; I was never told and always left out.

During the 2013 Christmas holiday, he gave everyone tickets to attend The Christmas Spectacular at the Radio City Music Hall where he worked, and again purposely left me out. Dexter wanted to stay home and keep me company, but I told him not to go against his father orders. I could have made his son go against him, but I knew better, so I did what I believe was right. Uncle Nathan was right; he wasn't my father. So as much as I wanted to blame him for making me feel unwanted, I blamed my father.

Even Acacia told Uncle Nathan how unfair he was sometimes. After refusing to take me out with his family, sometimes that same week he would ask me to run errands, and I completed all of his requests out of love. When they all came home one night, Uncle Nathan asked me to do him a favor, and the tasks he gave me weren't completed, and Granny found out the real reason why I wasn't going to the occasions he sent them on. UUncle Nathan had previously told Granny that every time he invited me, I refused. Dexter told her truthfully. Uncle Nathan was pissed off. He had borrowed money from me a long time ago, and then he went straight to the bank and returned, paying me back. I knew from that moment the best bone in him hated everything that concerned me. Instead of hating him, I looked on the bright side and used whatever bad he brought to the table as a stepping stone.

"Dexter, you're not doing what's expected of you, you know. You're following that jackass, and you're becoming a jackass just like him. Junior acts just like his father, and we don't want anything from his father. Let's teach this boy how to be a man and to do what is expected of real men. Can you do that for me and become a good man for Daddy?" said Uncle Nathan while I listened from the bedroom next door. When Dexter came out of the room to tell me, I stopped him.

"You don't have to tell me. I heard from the middle bedroom."

His face was sad, and then he cried.

That time I went into the closet where Dexter and I slept, and we talk about how fucked up Nathan was. Sometimes we would cry when I told him how much my grandparents loved me.

"Don't worry, Junior. Just now you'll be a famous artist and all your problems will be eliminated."

"Amen to that."

Dexter and I had some good times and still do. It's just that his father is not on good terms with me because of my father. But Dexter and I are good and will always be. For as long as I could remember, my mother said her father had put in for her to come to the United States, but living to see the day she came to New York was the next trouble I had coming.

After a few months, Dexter told me why his father stopped caring for me. My father and Uncle Nathan had gotten into an argument as a result of an altercation between my father and Kate. During their insulting curse out, my father told Uncle Nathan that he had to stop making Dexter and I to do all the work where we lived. I didn't know how my father found that out, but Uncle Nathan believed it was me.

"I don't mean to disrespect you, Junior, but your mother is a real fool," said Dexter.

"That's what I told you, right."

"She put would anyone's child in front of hers. Don't get me wrong, caring for someone else's child is great, but you have to love your child too."

"She's still the same woman, sitting back and talking a bunch of shit about me," I said.

Sometimes Uncle Nathan would sing to her about how much of a jackass I was, and my mother would laugh and agree with him to my face. Sometime it made me angry to the point where I wanted to tell her how much of an idiot I thought she was, but it would only make my grandmother's other hand fall, and I made her a promise. My mother was ridiculous after Nathan told her how stupid I was. Her job was to take in whatever Nathan exposed and share it with the people I was close to. Every day, my mother told me how much of a jackass I was not to see my father and to try to build a father–son relationship with him.

I sat in the closet for many hours, thinking about how much of a fucking cunt she was. Most of the times I saw red, but thanks to my creativity in drawing, painting, sculpting and writing that took all the negativity and brought forth anything positive—something that Amos Poe said, the man who would become my mentor.

On July 2013, Kate's relatives who lived in New Jersey were celebrating their family reunion. At first I didn't want to attend the family reunion because my father had refused to give me any of the tax return money he collected for me as his dependent, and there wasn't another way for me buy proper clothes. Kate really wanted me to attend the reunion, so at the last minute I decided to go.

There, I met Grace while being introduced to some of their relative. I didn't know Uncle Dave had gotten engaged to Grace until I saw a ring on his finger and asked him. Uncle Dave told me the ring was from his godmother, but if I wanted to know his business, he and Grace were together. Grace knew me before I knew her; she said around the time Kate and my father broke up, Kate told her about the way my father treated me. Grace had waited a long time to meet me. My grandmother said it just had to be the right time in order for me to meet her.

"So, how is school?" asked Grace.

"School is great," I replied.

"I heard you love to paint, draw, and write poems."

"Yeah, but I'm also taking on something new, learning how to make films."

"Wow! That sounds cool."

"I know."

"Do you know specifically what you what to do with film?" asked Grace

"I don't understand."

"You know, whether you want to act in or direct the film?"

"Oh! I want to be a screenwriter, director, and actor."

"Nice. Can I tell you something great?"

"What?" I replied curiously

"I've been working with this guy who's a really great filmmaker. His name is Johnny Rose. I'm going to give you his number so you can give him a call."

"Okay, when can I call him?"

"Call him tomorrow around ten in the morning. I'll tell him to expect your call. Tell him you're Grace's nephew, so he knows who you are, okay?"

"Got it."

"Now, go on and have some fun. We'll talk later."

I had to breathe for a few minutes because I was so

excited my oxygen had cut off. I felt like I was getting closer and closer to my dreams. Some fresh air would surely calm me down, but I was still excited.

The next morning before I called Johnny, I tried to look him up online. I saw that he is a New York City-based director and screenwriter. I couldn't wait, I called Johnny ten times at six in the morning when I woke, but his phone rang out. I continued every ten minutes until he answered my call at ten-thirty. Johnny Rose was leaving the country and wasn't going to return until August. Aunt Grace told me not to call back until August third, saying he would need a couple of days to relax and breathe.

On August 4, 2015, we scheduled an appointment where I would go over to his place and show him my work. Johnny fell in love with my drawings and paintings, but not the poems so much, as he's not very interested in poetry. We started talking about films, and I told him what I had learned at the Maysles Documentary Center. He then told me about the basic key points he learned over his years of filmmaking. Johnny said I might want to attend a college that had filmmaking as a major.

"Which school are you planning on attend?" asked Johnny.

"I don't know."

"You're going to college, right?"

"Yeah, I want to write a essay that talks about the

struggles and abuse I experienced in my home country."

"Where are you from?"

"Guyana, the land of many waters."

"Guyana, got it. What struggles and abuses did you face?"

For once in my life, someone was ready to listen.

I told Johnny a little bit of the relationship between my father and I from the time I was young and about the struggles my grandparents and I had, which were the main reasons why I came to America.

"You're in the right place at the right time. I'm glad to be part of your life, but I must congratulate you on the way you're dealing with your struggle. Don't judge your father or hold anything bad toward him. What you have to do is dig deep within yourself and be better than your father ever was." He paused. "I don't want you to only write an essay. I want you to write a book," said Johnny Rose.

I packed up my artwork, and we drank some iced tea he had in his refrigerator. While drinking the iced tea, I thought, A book? I can't write so much.

"Do you know how to write or read a script?" he asked.

"No."

"I'm going to give you the script for the movie Zero

Dark Thirty, which is an action film directed by Kathryn Bigelow and written by Mark Boal. Read ten pages of the script and watch ten minutes of the film, then read another ten pages and watch another ten minutes. When you're finished with the script and the movie, you should have an idea of how to write a movie script."

The following day, I met Aunt Grace and told her the good news. Instead of responding to the good news, Grace had someone else in mind for me to meet. His name is Anthony Rose, the son of Johnny Rose. After Anthony and I met, I started assisting him, which I loved. Anthony sat down with me and helped me fill out all of my college applications. He was pushing me to attend NYU, where he attended, or Columbia University, but I never believed I was smart enough to go there. I told Anthony those schools were too expensive, but he said I could get an art scholarship. I didn't believe him. Instead, I was more focused on writing my story.

I had to be careful because Lina might have told the good news to my father, which is why I didn't tell anyone in my school. Everyone thought I was going crazy because I was always happy, but they didn't know. Every day after school, I went over to Anthony's studio, where he had all of his drawings, paintings, and sculptures. My job was to help him carry and pick up artworks in Manhattan and sometimes clean the studio. It was often just the two of us in his 2012 Volvo, which he got from his mother, bumping to hip-hop and rap music either on Hot 97 or Power 105. Day by day, I told a little more of the horror I experienced with my father. When I noticed how disturbed it made him, we talked about how our dreams can and will turn out. While driving to his mother's house in Connecticut, I told him about the sexual abuse I survived.

He cried and didn't say anything for a while. Then, he said, "Don't worry, Ray. Everything is going to be fine. Your children will be happy to have you in their lives. All you have to do now is keep writing. It will help you, trust me. Everything might seem confusing right now, but it's going to change your life. All you have to do is finish the book, and it will take on a life of its own,"

"Can I tell you something?" I asked Anthony.

"Yeah, Ray, anything."

"Being with you guys and working toward the career I want is what makes me happy and keeps me going."

"Oh, Ray, don't worry, man. Just stay strong. Remember we love you more than anything and you're always welcome."

I thanked him and then said, "I don't mean to drown you in my problems, but it's my mother and the things she is doing. She's so evil, so wicked."

"Don't worry, man," he said, giving me a hug.

I didn't tell him what really went down because he

would have probably tried to call her. My mother told Kate and my father's household the reason I was visiting Grace was because I was having a sexual affair with her. One of my mother's cousins accused me of sleeping with some old woman. Their whole household said how ridiculous I was for having sex with my uncle's wife. When my mother was confronted by Grace, she told Grace that it was Kate and Granny who had spread the rumors, and that she didn't say anything. We didn't fall for her lies.

When I told Grace, she called my mother and asked her if she wanted her to get a definition of the character's test. I told Grace it was my mother lie because her household had known about it, and neither Kate nor Granny knew her or any of her family in New Jersey for any talking to have taken place. Two weeks later, my mother called Grace and told her Granny and Kate were still talking. My mother didn't know I had already investigated the matter and found out she was lying. Grace ignored her and told me she didn't want me to focus on their negative.

CHAPTER 22

Throughout the time my mother, Emma, and I was staying with Kate, I tried my best to keep Kate and Acacia
happy in every way I could. I had hoped they wouldn't
get mad at me because, as I told my mother, I had like
Erica. A few days after my mother, Emma, and I moved
into a Great Aunt's place in New Jersey, my mother told
me they found out. At first I tried to deny the relationship,
but she told me they made Erica confess. I was embarrassed, but words cannot accurately explain how I felt at
that point.

My mother and I didn't get along unless she wanted
something, so I knew someday, sooner or later, my grandmother was going to find out. When I spoke to my grandmother after my mother told me she knew about Erica
and my relationship, my grandmother acted as though she
wanted to question me about something. I wondered how

my grandmother felt about the situation; maybe I let her hands fall?

I didn't know what they told her, but I remembered how I had broke Kates heart for having an affair with her daughter. That night, Kate found out that I had liked Erica before she called my father to collect me. I know I had mess up big time and my father was going to kill me, but I was more concern about what her mother going to do to her. Kate sent me out of the room and kept Erica behind the closed door screaming and cursing at her. When my father came, I told him I forced Erica, she had nothing to do with it, but he didn't listen. He went into the room with Kate for a few minutes, then they all came out. Kate told my father, she didn't want me at her house and I left with Simon. I stood on the train thinking of what I had caused. I was overwhelmed. I returned to my father's house and my punishment continued. Immediately I exist my memories. I was bother and disturbed by my decisions.

CHAPTER 23

Two months before high school graduation, I had entered and applied for an art scholarship called, Art Is My... I had recently finished painted portrait based on the way I was feeling after brainstorming how I was going to start writing my story. I called the painting Art Is My Faith. In order to achieve something great or magnificent, you must have faith, even a little bit will take you somewhere, which is better than nowhere. The painting shows a human face with many colors and quotes that signify the path an individual will take once they have faith. My painting "Faith" is a painting of a human being's face, shoulder and upper chest bold in green across the head. In the brain printed white and red and written in black is: in order to achieve great things, we have to do mighty ones. In black and white on the cheeks of the face is, The truthful part of someone is within. The mouth has my faith written across it, Change begins when we speak positive.

Granny was always supportive of me and my art, and Erica never missed an event.

"Look on the bright side, you're about to graduate high school and move on to college," said Grace.

"For some reason, I'm not feeling the excitement."

"Why Junior?"

"When we look at schools and what I'm accomplishing and pursuing, I feel greater than words can explain, but family-wise everything seems corrupt," I said.

"I know. That's why I'm here. This was all planned out, and we will make it to the finish line. All I want you to do for me is to forget the problems they're putting you through and strive. You can and will do great things. You will inspire people who are down to stand tall. Just hold on, okay?" said Grace.

"Okay, Aunt Grace."

After she left for work that morning, I sat down and gave everything we discussed a thought, but no matter what I tried, my problems were drowning me. What must I do? Maybe it's not time to celebrate yet. I didn't have any intention to let down Aunt Grace, so I swallowed my self-pity and continued doing what was expected of me.

Every senior from Brooklyn College Academy, better

known as Legends of 2014, were given ten graduation tickets.

"Who was I going to give tickets to?" I asked myself when I first got my ten.

I knew I would give one to each Aunt Grace, Johnny, Anthony, and his youngest sister, Chelsea Rose, who I recently met. Both Katherine and Amber, Grace's daughters, told me that Kate, Granny, Erica, and my mother needed tickets. I didn't worry about my father's household because Lina had been given ten tickets as well. The night before my graduation, I slept in Brooklyn at Grace's apartment. My mother gossiped about how wrong I was to sleep there, but I couldn't have cared less. On the day of my graduation, some important appointments came up that made Aunt Grace unsure whether she was going to be present for the ceremony.

"Don't worry. I'll try to see if I can leave work early and get there. Okay, hun?"

"Okay."

"All I want you to think about is how much you have accomplished and what a marvelous day it will be. I have to go now. I'll see you later."

I couldn't blame her for something even my parents lacked.

How worse can today get? In two hours, I have to

start preparing for my graduation and there's a possibility Grace can't come. Holy shit, man, I thought.

Just after I stepped out of the bathroom, the phone rang. Erica called to say Granny couldn't make it. She had been called in for a job interview that she waited two weeks for on Long Island. Kate had a meeting at work and wasn't sure what time she was going to be free.

"I replaced Granny with Dexter and Mommy with Kasey," said Erica.

"Okay, that's fine."

"Before you hang up, where is the graduation?"

"Whitman Hall on BCA's campus. You can't miss it."

As it got closer to the time of my high school graduation, there wasn't any sign of Johnny, Anthony, or Chelsea. I borrowed my principal's phone and found out they were in a meeting and also didn't know what time they were going to be there.

A cab driver told me that my graduation would be the best day of my life. At first, I thought he was just telling me something nice because I was giving him a tip, but then most things fell into place. Erica, Kasey, Al, and Dexter showed up on behalf of Granny and Kate. On behalf of my father, his whole household came to support Lina.

"Y'all will go to an expensive restaurant and have a

belly full of food. Trust what I'm telling you," the cab driver said as I stepped out of the car.

"Amen," I replied.

In the lobby of Whitman Hall, most of my fellow graduates were introducing their parents and siblings to their friends. At the first opportunity I had, I ditched my parents and got in line to enter the building. My fellow graduates were happily talking, smiling, and kissing each other. The family, friends, and loved ones of my classmates cheered as we entered the building and walked on stage where the seats were placed. Before we took our seats, Ms. Jones asked us to join Juliet, another graduate, as she sang the national anthem. For the four years I attended Brooklyn College Academy with Juliet, I didn't know she had such an amazing voice. She brought tears to people's eyes. If I were blind, I would have thought Jennifer Hudson was giving us a special treat. Soon after she finished, it all began.

"First, I would love to thank the parents of these wonderful and educated young men and women. They did it, and I'm proud of them; we're all proud of them," said Mr. Pellum.

The audience cheered and gave a round of applause. There were a few announcements and jokes before the real deal took place. Ms. Jones was the first person to award the valedictorians. Juliet was one of ten students who took home the title of valedictorian. Ms. Roxy awarded two students for best sportsmanship. Ms. Becca gave out two awards for hardest worker in chemistry. Mr. Paul awarded one student for being the most improved student in math and another in English. Then Ms. Cole stood up.

"I met this young man who has grown to become extraordinarily gifted. When I first met him, he didn't know what he was capable of, but through his drawings, poems, paintings, and sculptures, he has uplifted lives and shown what an amazing person he has become. Inspired and motivated by his role models, such as Jean-Michel Basquiat, Spike Lee, Tyler Perry, Maya Angelou, Oprah Winfrey, and many more, he has proven to me, and soon the world, that this is just the start of his accomplishments. It is my honor to present the most improved and hardest worker award to Mr. Rayfield Walker."

The audience went wild with their cheering. Not one word on planet earth could express the way I felt. While walking to the front, my body shook and I was perspiring. I even accidentally stepped on a child's shoe. Every now and then, I close and open my eyes to make sure that moment was real.

Ms. Cole shook my hand and hugged me for a good thirty seconds. "You deserve it; and remember, this is only the beginning. There's more coming your way, just stay focused."

"Thank you so much," I replied.

Everyone, including the teaching staff, clapped, cheered, and screamed as I returned to my seat.

"Now, I'll hand the mic over to Mr. John to present the Phoenix award," said Ms. Cole. Murmurs went through the crowd, wondering what the award was for.

The Phoenix award is in recognition of someone's perseverance and hard work in overcoming obstacles throughout their education. Now, there are many students who suit the Phoenix award, but above all there is one individual who has proven himself identical to the phoenix for which this award is named.

"After immigrating from a small village in Guyana to the United States, this individual was not prepared for any of the hard work that came his way. But one of a few things I admire and will never forget is that throughout his failures, there was a room full of faith. Whenever he got a fifty-five, it motivated him to do better. When he got a sixty-five, it was celebrated like a ninety-five. With his faith and hard work, there soon were the seventies, which turned into seventy-fives, then eighties and eighty-fives. In his most recent college classes, he earned nineties and one hundred. I have been part of this young man's life and honored to see his creativity and skill. I view him as a Renaissance artist. Ladies and gentlemen, it's my pleasure to award the Phoenix to Rayfield Walker," said Mr. John.

I couldn't hold it in and on that day, I cried. The sounds from the crowd were uproarious. I didn't have any idea why they were cheering and clapping so loudly, but it sure made me feel wonderful. On my way to receive the Phoenix award, dizziness came over me. I stopped in the middle of the stage, wiped my face, and kept moving to shake hands and collect my prize. People said the most encouraging things.

"It's okay, hun."

"We love you!"

"He did it!"

"He proved himself."

"Go Rayfield! Go Rayfield!" cheered my classmates.

Again, I couldn't hold it in; I had to let some tears out.

"What, Ray? What is there not to achieve? You see what I was telling you all along? I know you could do this."

One thing you must remember: this is only the beginning, said the voice in my head.

In this life, no one knows what they will experience, accomplish, or even who they will become. I, The Jungle Boy, believe it is important to hold your head up high and never let your weaknesses to determine your future. This is only the beginning. Thank you to everyone who believed in me.

My father decided to take everyone, namely his father, Sabrina, Riya, Emma, Lina, and those who came from Kate's household, to lunch. I had never seen my father and grandfather so proud to acknowledge me as their own. Sadly, it was too late for them to get my attention or fool me into believing they actually love me. My father only pretended to show his love because of the rewards I received for all of my hard work. I went along with the phony act because Out of the Jungle was already in progress.

CPSIA information can be obtained
at www.ICGtesting.com
Printed in the USA
BVHW061218240920
589465BV00011B/535

9 781478 787136